Laptops

and

Literacy

Learning in the
Wireless Classroom

Laptops
and
Literacy

Learning in the Wireless Classroom

Mark Warschauer

Teachers College Press

Teachers College, Columbia University
New York and London

Published by Teachers College Press, 1234 Amsterdam Avenue, New York, NY 10027
Copyright © 2006 by Teachers College, Columbia University

Library of Congress Cataloging-in-Publication Data

Warschauer, Mark.
  Laptops and literacy: learning in the wireless classroom / Mark Warschauer
    p. cm.
  Includes bibliographical references and index.
  ISBN-13: 978-0-8077-4728-8 (hardcover)
  ISBN-10: 0-8077-4727-0 (hardcover)
  ISBN-13: 978-0-8077-4726-1 (pbk.)
  ISBN-10: 0-8077-4726-2 (pbk.)
  1. Education data—processing. 2. Computers and literacy.
I. Title
LB1028.43.W37 2006
428.0078′5—dc22   OCT 1 6 2007

2006017693

ISBN 13: 978-0-8077- 4726-1 (paper)   ISBN 10: 0-8077-4726-2 (paper)
ISBN 13: 978-0-8077-4727-8 (cloth)   ISBN 10: 0-8077-4727-0 (cloth)

Printed on acid-free paper
Manufactured in the United States of America
13 12 11 10 09 08 07 06   8 7 6 5 4 3 2 1

For Keiko, Danny, Mika, Noah, and (in memory) Mikey

Contents

Preface

This book is motivated by two fundamental beliefs. The first is that the rapid diffusion of new technologies is bringing about a shift in literacy practices as dramatic as any since the development of the printing press. The second is that U.S. public schools are a fundamentally conservative institution. Hundreds of school reform efforts have come and gone, but American secondary schools are still organized much as they were a century ago—students sitting quietly in rows and listening to teachers lecture in 50-minute periods. The resistance of schooling to change and, in particular, to adoption of new technologies was eloquently summarized by Larry Cuban in the title of his 1998 article, "Computer Meets Classroom: Classroom Wins."

What happens, then, when one of the most disruptive technologies of communication in history is placed in the hands of every student in a classroom, grade, or school? When the irresistible force, as it were, meets the immovable object? How do students' literacy practices in school change, or not change, when every student throughout the school day has a mobile personal computer wirelessly connected to the Internet?

This book attempts to address those questions. To do so, I examine theoretical conceptions of literacy, learning, and technology; consider prior research on technology and laptops in schools; and analyze data from a 2-year study of laptops and literacy practices in 10 diverse K–12 public schools in California and Maine.

The first two chapters will establish the overall terrain at issue. Chapter 1 will discuss conceptions of literacy in relationship to schooling and then define three major literacy challenges facing U.S. education today. Chapter 2 will discuss the role of technology in addressing these literacy challenges, outline why and how some schools have turned to one-to-one laptop computing programs, and introduce the laptops and literacy research study.

The next two chapters will consider the "traditional" literacies of reading and writing. Chapter 3 will examine the processes and outcomes of reading instruction in the laptop classroom, focusing in particular on the needs of culturally and linguistically diverse at-risk learners. Chapter 4 will examine the use of laptops in learning to write, examining both the proliferation and impact of what are considered to be authentic writing assignments, as well as the use of automated essay scoring in some laptop schools.

The next three chapters will address what are considered to be the "new" literacies of the twenty-first century and the thinking processes that enable them. Chapter 5 will consider information literacy and, more generally, how students in laptop classes approach research and knowledge construction. Chapter 6 will consider multimedia literacy and, in particular, the use of laptops for the creation of productions that involve multimodal resources (e.g., texts, sounds, music, images, video, animation). Chapter 7 will examine whether learning with laptops appears to be helpful in promoting the habits of mind that are required for literacy and learning in the twenty-first century, such as autonomy, flexibility, curiosity, and creativity.

Finally, Chapter 8 will summarize and conclude the book. It will re-examine the three main literacy challenges discussed in the first chapter and consider how these challenges are, or are not, addressed in the laptop classroom and what implications this has for teaching, program implementation, professional development, and research.

ACKNOWLEDGMENTS

Though the failings and shortcomings of this book are mine, the efforts of others helped make it possible. I am in particular indebted to the graduate and undergraduate students at the University of California, Irvine, who participated on the laptops and literacy research team: Michele Rousseau, Kelly Bruce, Doug Grimes, LaWanna Shelton, Melanie Wade, Jorge Velastegui, Kurt Suhr, Vanitha Chandrasekhar, Bryan Ventura, and Julia Nyberg. Paige Ware of Southern Methodist University also participated in the research team and has coauthored several papers with me related to this research. Her intellectual contributions have been invaluable. (I discuss in Chapter 2 how team members collaborated in collecting and analyzing data for this project. It is because of this team collaboration that I often use the plural pronoun *we* in referring to findings and interpretations in this book.)

Colleagues Henry Becker and Ann DeVaney from the Department of Education at the University of California, Irvine (UCI) have provided much sage advice. I also appreciate the collaboration of David Grant and Gabriel Del Real, who coauthored a paper that contributed to this study.

I am especially grateful to the administrators, teachers, students, and parents in California and Maine who welcomed us into their schools and homes. Though they must remain anonymous to protect the integrity of the study—pseudonyms have been used throughout—their support for this research was invaluable.

Funding for the study has been provided by the Ada Byron Research Center for Diversity in Computing and Information Technology (ABRC) and the Cultural Diversity Program of the Academic Senate Council on Research, Computing, and Library Resources, both at the University of California, Irvine. I am very grateful for the assistance of these two bodies and, in particular, for the support of Debra Richardson, Director of the ABRC and Dean of UCI's Donald Bren School of Information and Computer Science.

Bette Manchester, Director of Staff Development and Content for the State of Maine Learning Technology Initiative, and David Silvernail, professor and Director of the Center for Applied Research and Evaluation at the University of Southern Maine, were extremely helpful in providing information and insight about Maine's laptop program and suggestions about how to study it.

A team of undergraduate interviewers and transcribers also contributed valuably to the study. I am particularly thankful to Alvina Rosales for her work as an interviewer and translator and to Willis Wong for his able assistance in transcribing.

Finally, I thank Keiko, Danny, Mika, Noah, and (in memory) Mikey for their love and support, without which this effort would have been neither possible nor worthwhile.

CHAPTER I

Literacy Challenges of the Twenty-First Century

Literacy is a highly contested term, even more so in consideration of its relationship to new technologies. Just how contested was illustrated at a recent conference, when I heard a university professor explain how she had set up an after-school computer journalism club at a low-performing elementary school (see discussion of this project in Seiter, 2004). The 25 children who joined the club worked together to identify stories of interest, research them, and publish them in a newspaper that was circulated online and then printed and distributed for free to 15,000 community residents. The topics of newspaper stories varied between those of local community interest (such as local firefighters) and those related to popular culture (such as music or wrestling stars). The students quickly developed a variety of computer skills, including digital photography, keyboarding, and word processing, and also honed their reporting, writing, and editing talents.

Unfortunately, the school principal had problems with the project, since, as he told the professor, "This school is about literacy." It might seem odd that a journalism project such as this could be seen as contradictory to a school's focus on literacy. But the principal and professor obviously had very different conceptions of literacy in mind. The principal's main concern was that the at-risk students at his low-performing school develop the reading and language arts proficiencies measured on annual high-stakes exams, and he apparently saw little evidence that the project would contribute to that goal. The professor sought to develop the kinds of reading, writing, language, research, and media skills she believes are required in today's world.

I am not unsympathetic to the principal's position. After all, the fate of his school largely depends on how quickly he can raise test scores, and sometimes single-mindedness helps in that pursuit. It is also true that many proponents of empowering students with new technology

1

too often overemphasize the excitement involved and underemphasize the types of rigorous instruction required for at-risk students to learn (e.g., see my critique of the Indian Hole-in-the-Wall project in Warschauer, 2003a; Warschauer, 2003b). However, in the long run I believe that these two goals—teaching students the basics and helping them master the exciting new ways of communicating that are relevant to twenty-first-century life—are fully compatible, and I further believe that technology can play a critical role in that process. To understand why this is the case, it is necessary to examine what literacy entails and what literacy challenges U.S. schools face today.

DEFINING LITERACY

Literacy is commonly thought of as the ability to decode and encode words on a page. From this perspective, literacy is context-free and value-neutral, located in the mind of individuals, and usually acquired in the first few years of school, mainly through the mastery of phonics.

There are several problems with this view of literacy. First, application of phonetic principles is just one of a wide variety of skills that readers use in order to decode words, and knowing how to decode words is just one piece of a much broader process of getting and making meaning from and with texts. Luke and Freebody (1999) suggest that literacy involves four sets of overlaying practices:

Break the code of texts: recognizing and using the fundamental features of written texts including alphabet, sounds in words, spelling, and patterns of sentence structure

Participate in the meanings of text: understanding and composing meaningful written, multimodal, and spoken texts from within the meaning systems of particular cultures, institutions, or communities

Use texts functionally: traversing the social relations around texts; knowing about and acting on the different cultural and social functions that texts perform, and knowing that these functions shape the way texts are structured

Critically analyze and transform texts: understanding and acting on the knowledge that texts are not neutral, that they represent particular views and silence other points of view, that they influence people's ideas, and that they can be critiqued and redesigned in novel ways

In addition, because such meaning making is highly context dependent, literacy is not a singular but rather a plural construct. There are many types of literacy for different situations. To use texts functionally in one setting, such as an Islamic madrassa in Pakistan, is very different from using texts functionally in another setting, such as a medical school in the United States (for a description of diverse literacy practices by members of the Vai tribe in Liberia, see Scribner & Cole, 1981). Scholars thus often refer to the notion of literacies rather than simply literacy. In this book, I am especially concerned with two sets of literacy practices: academic and digital.

Academic Literacies

Academic literacies refer to the literacy practices or competencies that allow people to succeed in academic work in schools and universities. The most complete analysis and description of academic literacy was published by a group of faculty from California's public higher education system (Intersegmental Committee of the Academic Senates, 2002). The document, reflecting college faculty's expectations of student competency, is a good indication of how far beyond simple decoding a student must go to be fully literate in an academic environment. It focuses on four main areas: reading and writing, listening and speaking, habits of mind, and technology use.

Reading and writing competencies range from the fairly basic, such as retaining information or identifying main ideas, to the more complex, such as understanding the rules of various genres, anticipating where arguments or narratives are heading, and correctly documenting research materials. Listening and speaking competencies range from identifying digressions and illustrations to seriously interrogating diverse views, and are supplemented by additional competencies specified for nonnative speakers of English, such as recognizing the spoken form of vocabulary previously encountered only in written form.

Perhaps the most interesting set of competencies are referred to as "habits of mind." These include the ability to sustain and express intellectual curiosity, experiment with new ideas, exercise persistence in pursuing difficult tasks, and respect principles as well as experiences. The fact that such habits of mind are listed first in the report reinforces how central they are viewed by these faculty to a framework of academic literacy.

The final set of competencies addressed by the report are in the technological realm and include items such as using search engines effectively, evaluating material found online, and consulting experts via e-mail.

Digital Literacies

The technological competencies specified in the California report overlap with a second realm of literacy practices often termed *digital* or *electronic literacies.* Various groups and individuals define these differently, but in general the terms refer to ways of making meaning from and interpreting texts in computer-based digital realms. I have previously categorized these as consisting of four sets of overlapping literacies (Warschauer, 2003b):

1. *Computer literacy* refers to the general fluency and comfort in navigating around and using a computer. Though the concept of computer literacy is often critiqued—and deservedly so—as being too minimalist as a curricular goal in schools, it is nonetheless true that computer literacy has a high impact on successful participation in today's world. For example, even such a renowned scholar as Gabriel Garcia Marquez, arguably one of the most literate people in the world, readily pointed out how much more productive he became once he learned to use a computer (see discussion in Day & Miller, 1990; Warschauer, 2003b).
2. *Information literacy* refers to the ability to determine the extent of information needed, access needed information effectively and efficiently, evaluate information and its sources critically, incorporate selected information into one's knowledge base, use information effectively to accomplish a specific purpose, and access and use information ethically and legally (American Library Association, 2000).
3. *Multimedia literacy* refers to the ability to interpret and create products using a variety of digitized semiotic resources, including texts, typography, images, sounds, and video.
4. *Computer-mediated communication literacy* (CMC literacy) refers to the interpretation and writing skills necessary to communicate effectively via online media. At a simple level, this includes the "netiquette" of polite online communication. At a more advanced level, it includes the pragmatics of effective argumentation and persuasion in various sorts of Internet media. At the most advanced level, CMC literacy includes knowing how to establish and manage online communications for the benefit of groups of people.

Certain types of digital literacy overlap strongly with scholarly goals and purposes, thus accounting for their inclusion within academic literacy frameworks such as that described above. This is particularly true of tasks related to finding, evaluating, and using online sources of information. To attempt to norm and measure academically related digital literacies, particularly those associated with finding and using information, Educational Testing Service (2004) has developed the *ICT [Information and Communications Technology] Literacy Assessment,* which is now being made available to educational institutions across the country. Other types of digital literacy practices, such as instant messaging, are viewed by many as less relevant or even contradictory to the mastery of academic literacy. In summary, academic and digital literacies are viewed as overlapping in some ways and conflicting in others. The relationship and tension between these two sets of literacies will be a theme of this book.

A LITERACY CRISIS?

It is often said that U.S. schools are facing a literacy crisis. Yet as Mc-Quillan (1998) points out, U.S. students are not among the worst readers in the world, there is no epidemic of reading disabilities, and children are reading at the same or better level than they did a generation or two ago. Indeed, reading test scores among younger children have even ticked up a notch or two in recent years (National Center for Educational Statistics, 2005).

However, while we may not be facing a literacy *crisis,* we are certainly facing sobering literacy *challenges,* and we can take little comfort in the fact that reading levels are no worse now than in previous generations. Simply put, the context of literacy has changed dramatically in the United States in the last 50 years, and what may have been acceptable previously is no longer so now. In the remainder of this chapter, I will outline the three main literacy challenges faced in today's schools—labeled (1) *past and future,* (2) *home and school,* and (3) *rich and poor*—and this book will explore the potential of laptop computer programs to help address these challenges.

Past and Future

The first literacy challenge involves the changes that have occurred in literacy requirements of American society in the past 50 years, with respect to sites, tools, and functions.

In the post–World War II period, there was great concern with achieving *functional literacy,* which was defined as being able to read and fill out a job application. There was a logic to that definition because, in the economy of that time, being able to fill out an application may have been a sufficient literacy level to get and keep a stable, unionized job in an automobile factory, steel plant, or machine shop.

Now, a half century later, those jobs have for the most part disappeared, as the manufacturing sector of the workforce has decreased from 32% in the 1940s to 13% today (Forbes, 2004), and the percentage of unionized workers has fallen by the same degree (from 35% to less than 13%: Joyce, 2005). And these trends are accelerating. Of the 21.6 million new jobs being created between 2002 and 2012, fully 20.8 million are expected to be in the service sector, with the largest job growth in areas such as education and health services (to grow by 31.8%); professional and business services (to grow by 30.4%); and information services, including telecommunications, broadcasting, and publishing (to grow by 18.5%). Meanwhile, employment is projected to continue declining in manufacturing, agriculture, and mining (Bureau of Labor Statistics, 2005). Simply put, the prototypical U.S. work site is shifting from the factory to the office, where even many entry-level positions in the new economy require more diverse and exacting forms of literacy than those needed for well-paying manufacturing positions of two generations ago.

Meanwhile, the jobs that drive our knowledge economy and provide people with power, prestige, and high pay are almost all in what former secretary of labor Robert Reich (1991) called "symbolic analyst services." According to Reich, symbolic analysts "solve, identify, and broker problems by manipulating symbols." They "simplify reality into abstract images that can be rearranged, juggled, experimented with, communicated to other specialists, and then, eventually, transformed back into reality" (p. 178). They include research scientists, design engineers, software engineers, biotechnology engineers, sound engineers, public relations executives, lawyers, real estate developers, management consultants, financial consultants, energy consultants, architectural consultants, management information specialists, organization development specialists, strategic planners, systems analysts, advertising executives, marketing strategists, art directors, architects, cinematographers, film editors, production designers, publishers, writers, editors, journalists, television and film producers, and professors.

Symbolic analysts must be highly analytic in their use of information, persuasive and creative in their communications, and autonomous and flexible in their ability to manage tasks from a number of simultaneous projects. Most symbolic analysts use digital technology on a constant basis to network with others, seek or analyze information, and create multimedia products for diverse audiences. Symbolic analysts—and indeed other workers in a knowledge economy—must be highly adaptive, as the single lifetime job that many workers enjoyed in the twentieth century is a thing of the past. Rather, people must constantly reinvent themselves, adopt new identities, and develop new skills in a rapidly changing job market, becoming what Gee (2004) has called "shape-shifting portfolio people." As Gee explains,

> Shape-shifting portfolio people . . . see themselves in entrepreneurial terms. That is, they see themselves as free agents in charge of their own selves as if those selves were projects or businesses. They believe they must manage their own risky trajectories through building up a variety of skills, experiences, and achievements in terms of which they can define themselves as successful now and worthy of more success later. Their set of skills, experiences, and achievements, at any one time, constitutes their portfolio. However, they must also stand ready and able to rearrange these skills, experiences, and achievements creatively (that is, to shape-shift into different identities) in order to define themselves anew (as competent and worthy) for changed circumstances. If I am now an "X," and the economy no longer needs "X"s, or "X"s are no longer the right thing to be in society, but now "Y"s are called for, then I have to be able to shape-shift quickly into a "Y." (p. 105)

Meanwhile, the societal tools of literacy have also changed radically in the last 50 years, as reading, writing, and research move rapidly from the page to the screen. Fully 70% of Americans used the Internet on a typical day in 2004, up from just 45% four years previously. Some 2 trillion email messages were sent in the U.S. in 2004 (eMarketer, 2004), and email has long surpassed face-to-face and telephone interaction as the main form of communication in many U.S. businesses (American Management Association International, cited in Warschauer, 2000b). Some 50 million Americans read blogs in the first quarter of 2005, up from 34 million a year previously (ComScore Networks, 2005). And the Internet has become a main source of news, shopping, entertainment, and socializing for tens of millions of Americans (Rainie & Horrigan, 2005).

This represents not just a shift of site or tool, but also of function, as witnessed by four revolutionary features of information and communications technology (ICT) as it applies to literacy. First, ICT allows *interactive written communication* as evidenced in instant messaging, chat, and email. These bridge the historic divide between speech (traditionally used for interactive communication) and writing (tradition-

ally used to record experience and interpret and reflect on meaning;
see discussion in Warschauer, 1997). Second, it allows the creation of
hypertexts, challenging traditional forms of narrative and bringing together information in entirely new ways. Third, it democratizes *multimedia creation*, allowing the easy combination of text, image, sounds,
and video, and thus challenging the dominance of the written word in
many professional, training, and academic contexts. Fourth, it allows
a global form of *many-to-many communication*, as witnessed by the
growing popularity of blogs and their increasing impact on journalism,
politics, and personal expression.

In summary, the sites, tools, and societal requirements of literacy
have gone through dramatic changes in the last half century, leading one
prominent cognitive scientist to describe computer-mediated communication as representing the fourth revolution in human communication,
cognition, and the production of knowledge, following the prior revolu-
tions of the development of language, writing, and print (Harnad, 1991).

These dramatic socioeconomic and technological changes have
helped reshape almost every institution in the United States, from
businesses to health care to politics. Yet schooling remains, in many
ways, unchanged. A visitor to many U.S. high schools today would witness a similar site to that of a half century ago: some 30–35 students
sitting in rows for a 50-minute period, passively listening to a teacher's
lecture. Student participation in class is highly controlled, with almost
all interaction falling within a pattern known as IRE, starting with a
teacher's Initiation, followed by a student's Response, and then ending
with a teacher's Evaluation (Mehan, 1985).

The current emphasis on high-stakes testing complicates efforts
at modernizing education. While holding the bar high for all students is an admirable goal, placing such high stakes on a narrow set
of assessments has had the unfortunate effect of discouraging efforts
at developing critical thinking or creatively using new technologies
(e.g., see Warschauer, Knobel, & Stone, 2004). Instead, administrators
and teachers adopt scripted approaches involving basal reading series,
worksheets, and drills, and fear straying from testable content even to
pursue highly promising teaching and learning moments. At the same
time, courses such as music and art, which are believed to have positive effects on students' creativity and cognition, are eliminated from
school budgets as limited resources are redirected toward intensified
instruction in the testable subjects of language arts and math.

These problems plague not only our worst schools but also our best
ones. Academic instruction for the top students at elite high schools in
the United States is dominated by Advanced Placement (AP) courses,
which give students a competitive edge in gaining admission to top-

notch universities (see discussion in Warschauer, 2003b). However, AP classes are usually "a mile high and an inch deep" (Landsberg & Rathi, 2005, p. B1), since they attempt to cover a vast amount of material in preparation for the tests. A principal at a private school that is eliminating AP instruction explained that his school and faculty "prefer courses that prepare students to be reflective, analytical and ongoing learners. Classes geared to a specific, externally designed test do not best achieve this objective" (Landsberg & Rathi, 2005, p. B1). However, only a tiny handful of schools are dropping AP courses. The main trend is that public schools throughout the country are adding more AP courses, as such courses are seen as the gold standard of high school instruction.

What then might a school curriculum tailored to the needs of twenty-first-century life look like? A number of models have been put forward in the United States (e.g., Partnership for 21st Century Skills, 2003) and internationally (for a review, see Leu, Donald, Kinzer, Coiro, & Cammack, 2004). A particularly cogent model—and one that brings together the concepts of many other models as well—has been developed by the North Central Regional Educational Laboratory and the Metiri Group (2003). That framework, referred to as enGauge, specifies four sets of skills that are required of twenty-first-century learners: digital-age literacy, inventive thinking, effective communication, and high productivity (see Table1.1).

Of course, learning cannot be reduced to skills and competencies; it must be centered on content. But mastery of content is best achieved through collaborative critical inquiry and in-depth analysis of challenging problems related to that content, not through memorization for exams. Thus the skills and competencies described above and the need for mastery of content in science, social studies, literature, and other areas are fully compatible. But orienting instruction in such a direction is not easy, especially in the mass institutions of public schools. This then is the first main literacy challenge for K–12 education: how schools can become more relevant by teaching the kinds of literacy, thinking, communication, and productivity skills, as well as academic content, needed in twenty-first-century life.

Home and School

The same media and social changes discussed above have led to a second challenge facing educational institutions today: how to overcome the gap between home and school. Actually, U.S. schools have long had difficulty valuing and leveraging the funds of knowledge that diverse students bring from their home and community (Gonzales,

Table 1.1. Twenty-First-Century Literacies

EnGauge 21st-Century Skills	
Digital-age literacy	• Basic, scientific, economic, and technological literacies • Visual and information literacies • Multicultural literacy and global awareness
Inventive thinking	• Adaptability, managing complexity, and self-direction • Curiosity, creativity, and risk taking • Higher order thinking and sound reasoning
Effective communication	• Teaming, collaboration, and interpersonal skills • Personal, social, and civic responsibility • Interactive communication
High productivity	• Prioritizing, planning, and managing for results • Effective use of real-world tools • Ability to produce relevant, high-quality products

Moll, & Amanti, 2005). I will return to the issue of the cultural and linguistic resources that students have, and how they are or are not valued in school, in the following section. For now, though, I want to focus on a particular type of mismatch, that related to the use of new media at home.

An interesting portrayal of teenagers' changing home media use and literacy practices is provided by Miller (2002), who documents the lives of two middle-class white teenagers: Horace, in 1946, and JimJim, in 2001. Horace, as a post–World War II teen, is wrapped up in the grand narratives of books, from *Alice and Wonderland* to *Wuthering Heights* to Dostoyevsky's *Notes from the Underground*, of which all helped shape his identity. And even beyond books, Horace's whole world was immersed in paper, from his mawkish diary to his love letters to his handwritten examinations.

JimJim, in contrast, lives in an emerging posttypographic era. Jim-Jim rarely reads books. Instead, he spends virtually all his free time at his computer, usually doing five or six things at once: playing a multiplayer online game called SubSpace with people from various countries, listening to MP3 songs, sending email to friends around the world, instant-messaging with other friends, engaging in a multiperson chat, and completing homework assignments. Of these various activities, SubSpace plays a particularly prominent role. JimJim has risen up through the ranks to become a SuperModerator ("Smod") in SubSpace, and his job includes "enforcing the rules, watching for cheaters, hosting events, things like that" (Miller, 2002). The SubSpace community provides many of the contacts for his other forms of online communication.

Though both Horace and JimJim could be among the literate elite of their times, their literacy practices were clearly different. Besides the physical difference of paper and screen, several other important differences emerge. First, Horace's literacy practices take place one at a time, through deep involvement in separate reading or writing tasks. JimJim, instead, multitasks, carrying out numerous literacy activities at once. Second, Horace's literacy is, to a considerable degree, private, whereas JimJim's literacy activities involve intense and passionate engagement with other people. This engagement brings JimJim in communication with diverse communities of people throughout the world. Third, whereas Horace's reading tends to be contemplative and reflective, JimJim's computer activities are highly interactive and fast-paced. Miller points out that "a tremendous amount of linguistic exuberance and creativity is required for the various uses of the Web JimJim habitually makes, day after day, for many hours a day." For JimJim, this interactivity involves not only remaking language, but also refashioning himself, as he adopts numerous identities in the course of playing SubSpace and engaging in other online activities.

JimJim is a perfect illustration of what Howe and Strauss (2000) call "Millennials," a generation born after 1982 who have grown up as "native" users of new digital technologies. Millennials have grown up with the Internet, and they use it creatively and autonomously. For example, a study by Levin and Arafeh (2002), based on interviews with school children across the country, documents a growing "digital disconnect" between students' uses of the Internet at home and school. Their study suggests that "for the most part, students' educational use of the Internet occurs outside of the school day, outside of the school building, outside the direction of their teachers" (p. iii). They describe a number of ways that children make use of the Internet at home, including (1) as a virtual textbook and reference library (to find primary and secondary source materials for reports, presentations, and projects); (2) as a virtual study group (to collaborate on project work with classmates and study together for tests and quizzes); (3) as a virtual locker, backpack, and notebook (to keep track of their work and assignments); and (4) as a virtual guidance counselor (to gather information related to schools, careers, and postsecondary education). Children report that

Internet use at school is much more restricted, due to limited access, restrictive policies, or uninspiring assignments.

Millennials also play video games. And while the themes of their games are not always as wholesome as parents would like, the cognitive challenges built into many popular video games provide excellent opportunities for learning. Literacy theorist and cognitive psychologist Jim Gee (2003), after studying video games for several years, put together a list of 36 learning principles embedded in video games that are absent from most classrooms. Here I summarize the 12 I consider the most important:

1. *The Active, Critical Learning Principle*: All aspects of the learning environment are set up to encourage active and critical, not passive, learning.
2. *Semiotic Principle*: Learning about and coming to appreciate interrelations within and across multiple sign systems (images, words, actions, symbols, and artifacts) as a complex system is core to the learning experience.
3. *Achievement Principle*: For learners of all levels of skill there are intrinsic rewards from the beginning, customized to each learner's level, effort, and growing mastery and signaling the learner's ongoing achievements.
4. *Practice Principle*: Learners get lots of practice in a context where the practice is not boring (i.e., in a virtual world that is compelling to learners on their own terms and where the learners experience ongoing success). They spend lots of time on task.
5. *Regime of Competence Principle*: Learners get ample opportunity to operate within, but at the outer edge of, their resources, so that at those points things are felt as challenging, but not "undoable."
6. *Probing Principle*: Learning is a cycle of probing the world (doing something); reflecting in and on this action and, on this basis, forming a hypothesis; reprobing the world to test this hypothesis; and then accepting or rethinking the hypothesis.
7. *Multiple Routes Principle*: There are multiple ways to make progress. This multiplicity allows learners to make choices and rely on their own strengths and styles of learning and problem solving, while exploring alternative styles.
8. *Bottom-up Basic Skills Principle*: Basic skills are not learned in isolation or out of context; rather, what counts as a basic skill is discovered bottom up by engaging in more and more

of the game or games like it.

9. *Just-in-Time Principle*: The learner is given explicit information both on demand and just in time, when the learner needs it or just at the point where the information can best be understood and used in practice.

10. *Discovery Principle*: Overt telling is kept to a minimum, allowing ample opportunity for the learner to experiment and make discoveries.

11. *Transfer Principle*: Learners are given both ample opportunity to practice and support for transferring what they have learned earlier to later problems, including problems that require adapting and transforming that earlier learning.

12. *Insider Principle*: The learner is an "insider," "teacher," and "producer" (not just a "consumer"), able to customize the learning experience and game from the beginning and throughout the experience.

Finally, millennials are multimodal learners. Like previous generations of youth, millennials love music, but they have far more options than did previous generations to select their music, creatively combine or package music, listen to music throughout the day, digitally edit their music, or integrate music in with other media. Similarly, they are the first generation to grow up in the era of digital photography and video, and they take for granted downloading, cropping, and sharing digital images and integrating images or video into reports, presentations, and other productions.

Of course, not all media activity by youth is unproblematic or a perfect match for promoting academic literacy. A fascination with images and music can supplant interest in written texts. The ease of finding information on the Internet can often result in copyright violation or plagiarism. And video games seldom focus on topics of academic content. Overcoming the home-school disconnect related to new media use is thus not an easy task. But other institutions, from the military to businesses, have made greater strides in integrating new media into instruction and thus more effectively reaching the millennial generation. Schools have much room for improvement in this regard.

Rich and Poor

The third challenge refers to the shameful stratification in American education according to socioeconomic status (SES), race, ethnicity, and language. This stratification begins with the unequal resources that diverse groups bring to schooling, with children of well-to-do families starting with a vast advantage due to the social, cultural, and financial capital of their families (Bourdieu & Passeron, 1986). It is then amplified through unequal educational inputs, with schools in low-income neighborhoods receiving less funding and having fewer resources or fully qualified teachers than schools in high-income neighborhoods (Brown et al., 2005; Kozol, 1991; Sunderman & Kim, 2005). The result is extreme disparities in test score outcomes and graduation rates, with roughly half of Black and Latino students failing to achieve even basic reading proficiency or to graduate from high school (see Table 1.2).

Overcoming socioeconomic and racial gaps in education has been a perennial challenge in the United States; now, however, disparities in education and literacy have a much greater impact on people's life opportunities. For example, in 1975 the average person with an advanced degree earned twice as much as a high school dropout, but by 1999 the amount was greater than 3.7 times as much. Those entering the workforce with a bachelor's, master's, or professional degree today are expected to earn $1.1 million, $1.5 million, or $3.4 million more, respectively, than a high school dropout over a 40-year career (Day & Newburger, 2002). A total of 49 out of the 50 highest paying jobs in the United States now require a bachelor's degree or higher, with the sole exception being that of air traffic controller (Bureau of Labor Statistics, 2005). Disparities of education and social opportunity, as well as changing economic circumstances, mean that the United States is now much more unequal, and more hazardous for the poor, than even just a few decades ago, whether measured by income disparity, wealth disparity, opportunities for social mobility, or number of people lacking medical insurance (Lardner & Smith, 2006).

The other major factor contributing to the rise of educational, social, and economic inequality is immigration patterns. These same socioeconomic changes that have reduced job stability in the United States and elsewhere have also brought about demographic shifts, as increasing numbers of workers cross borders in search of economic opportunity. The United States now has both the largest annual immigration flow and the highest number of immigrants in its history, with the percentage of immigrants among the total population higher than any time in the last 60 years (Fix & Passel, 2001; Rytina, 2005). Urban school districts in California, Texas, New York, and elsewhere often have a majority of students who are first- or second-generation immigrants from non-English-speaking countries. In California, for example, 46% of the K–12 public school population is Latino and another 11.1% is of Asian or Pacific Islander origin; more than 25% of the state's student population is classified as English language learn-

Table 1.2. Racial Disparities in U.S. Education

	Eighth-grade students reading at basic level	Students graduating high school
White	83%	75%
Asian/Pacific Islander	79%	77%
Hispanic	56%	53%
Black	54%	50%

Sources: Donahue, Daane, & Grigg, 2003; Orfield, Losen, Wald, & Swanson, 2004.

ers (Ed-Data, 2005). Latino immigrants are also relocating throughout the country. Between 1990 and 2000, the most dramatic increases in Latino population occurred in southern states, including North Carolina (394%), Arkansas (337%), Georgia (300%), Tennessee (278%), and South Carolina (211%; Population Reference Bureau, 2004).

As a result of these immigration patterns and the concentration of Latinos in high-poverty communities, the earlier dream of Black–White integration in schools has been replaced by a reality in which most Blacks and Latinos go to schools where relatively few Whites attend (Frankerberg, Lee, & Orfield, 2003). While exceptions exist, these majority–minority schools are noted for low expectations, an unchallenging curriculum, and punitive behavioral controls (Kozol, 1991). It is thus not surprising that the graduate rate from typical urban schools is low, and that even fewer of these graduates go on to graduate from college or become "symbolic analysts."

In an increasingly globalized economy, the presence of large numbers of immigrants with specialized cultural and linguistic knowledge should in theory be a resource for the country. Unfortunately, one aspect of the home-school disconnect described above has been a persistent unwillingness to value linguistic diversity and home language resources (see discussion in Vásquez, Pease-Alvarez, & Shannon, 1994). For example, a recent meta-analysis of bilingual vs. English-only education found a clear advantage for the former in improving English language reading ability of Spanish-speaking students, not to mention fostering and maintaining Spanish language literacy (Slavin & Cheung, 2005). This is to be expected, given the long-known cognitive benefit of first learning to read in one's own language and then transferring that skill to a second language (Cummins, 1991). Yet in spite of the educational benefits of bilingual education, the practice is increasingly shunned in favor of less effective English-only approaches. Meanwhile, our nation suffers from a death of well-educated biliterate adults who can conduct global business in two languages.

This failure of our educational system to fully educate its diverse population has serious negative social and economic consequences, especially for the individuals who suffer from substandard education but also for our nation as a whole. This was cogently illustrated when Toyota Motor Corporation recently turned its back on hundreds of millions of dollars of subsidies offered by several American states in favor of building an automobile plant in Ontario, Canada, citing as a major reason the fact that Canadian workers are easier and less expensive to train than their U.S. counterparts.

The federal government's No Child Left Behind Act (NCLB) of 2001 was designed ostensibly to address the problem of underperformance in U.S. schools. Though high-stakes test regimes such as NCLB sometimes succeed in raising test scores, their overall effectiveness for improving education has been called into question, as witnessed by the results of the Texas Assessment of Academic Skills (TAAS) program, launched in 1990–91. Independent analysis of TAAS results indicates that much of the state's highly touted test score gains are attributed to pushing low-performing students into special education programs, which are not counted in schools' accountability ratings, or even out the door, with only 50% of minority students in Texas advancing from Grade 9 to high school graduation in the first decade of the program (Haney, 2000). In addition, the gains reported on TAAS were far out of proportion to Texas students' gains on national tests, suggesting that they were due to teaching to the test in the most narrow fashion (Klein, Hamilton, McCaffrey, & Stecher, 2000) while resources were diverted from more promising educational initiatives (McNeil & Valenzuela, 2001).

Reeves (2002) has gathered data on what he calls "90/90/90 schools," defined as schools that have large numbers of low-income and minority students and are achieving high academic performance. He attributes such success in part to high academic standards and expectations. In addition, these high-performing high-poverty schools pay a great deal of attention to assessment, but not necessarily to the annual district and state assessments. Rather, weekly assessments of student progress are constructed and administered by classroom teachers. As Reeves explains, "the consequence of students performing badly was not an admonishment to 'Wait until next year' but rather the promise that 'You can do better next week'"(p. 189). Students in these schools spend a good deal of time on in-depth learning rather than trying to cover numerous curricular objectives. In addition, the schools all placed a high emphasis on informative student writing (a point that will be discussed in Chapter 4).

Regrettably, the types of schools that Reeves describes are few and far between. Instead, large numbers of schools in low-SES communities are being labeled as *failing* under NCLB regulations, and depressing numbers of students in these schools are failing to achieve basic literacy and dropping out of school.

THE HOPE OF TECHNOLOGY

In summary, though there is no new literacy crisis in the United States, there are substantial literacy challenges, and socioeconomic developments of the past few decades have made these challenges more daunting. Yet the same technologies that have helped transform the economy and society also show promise for helping address the literacy challenges that have arisen (e.g., see positive assessments of technology and learning in after-school programs in Hull & Nelson, 2005; Mayer, Blanton, Duran, & Schustack, 1999; Vásquez, 2002). Improved integration of technology in schooling is obviously a key element of tackling both of the first two challenges described above—updating curriculum and instruction from the past to the future and overcoming the strong home-school disconnect in how children learn. Many believe that technology in schools can also be a lever for overcoming inequality between students in rich and poor communities, by giving low-SES students powerful learning tools that can help them leapfrog out of educational disadvantage. The following chapter will examine whether educational technology has fulfilled its promise, and why increasing numbers of educators are turning to one-to-one laptop programs as an alternative approach.

CHAPTER 2

Educational Computing's Third Wave

Over the last 100 years, one new technology after another has been introduced into schools with the promise of revolutionizing education. Yet, as Larry Cuban (1986) points out, neither film nor radio nor television fulfilled marketers' promises that these new media would transform how children learn in school. Instead, each of these technologies was relegated to the margins of classroom instruction, usually used for at most an hour a week for a special activity.

When seen in this trajectory, the future of computers in education looks bleak. Indeed, Cuban, the preeminent U.S. historian of technology in education, does believe that computers will suffer the same fate, and he has some data to back up his view (Cuban, 2001).

However, it would be a mistake to consider film, radio, and television as the only technologies that have been previously introduced into classrooms. Other technologies, such as pencils, paper, pens, books, and blackboards are ubiquitous in schools, and have been used so frequently and so long that they are no longer thought of as technologies at all. The question, then, is whether computers and the Internet, in relationship to education, are more like a film projector or are more like books, paper, and pens. We can start to answer that question through a brief overview of computers in education.

THE FIRST WAVE: TEACHING MACHINES

The first wave of educational computing had its roots in the late 1950s, when behaviorist B. F. Skinner first developed teaching machines for programmed instruction (Johnstone, 2003). In 1959 the dean of engineering at the University of Illinois, Urbana-Champaign, convened a committee to examine the broader prospects of teaching machines in education. The chairman of the committee consulted with a graduate student, Don Bitzer, who then built a primitive machine for computer-assisted instruction based on a television monitor, a keyboard, and a connection to a university mainframe. Bitzer entitled his system "Programmed Logic for Automatic Teaching Operations," and it has since been known by its acronym, PLATO (Johnstone, 2003).

The goal of PLATO, and of the broader first wave of educational computing that it represented, was to serve as a *tutor* to students, allowing them to learn material at their own pace by proceeding through a series of computerized drills while sitting at terminals connected to a mainframe. Though PLATO eventually received millions of dollars of support from the National Science Foundation and was used in schools from the 1960s to the mid-1980s, it never achieved a mass presence, due in part to its great expense.

THE SECOND WAVE: COMPUTERS AS TOOLS

A second wave of educational technology spread in the 1980s, following the development and diffusion of the personal computer. Though computers continued to be used as tutors, educators increasingly also viewed the computer as a *tool*. According to this new vision, children would no longer complete computerized drills but would instead use computers as an instrument of their own productivity and creativity. Popular tool-like activities included writing and revision with word processing software and programming of on-screen turtles or actual Lego robots using the Logo programming language.

This notion of computing as tool has two underlying beliefs. On the one hand, computer use was seen as a powerful way to engage students' minds. Seymour Papert, the father of the Logo Turtle project (and a protégé of educational psychologist Jean Piaget), argued that "education has very little to do with explanation, it has to do with engagement, with falling in love with the material" (Papert, 1980, p. viii). Alan Kay, a computer scientist who helped conceive of both the graphical user interface and the laptop computer, explained the matter in more detail:

> The intensely interactive and involving nature of the personal computer seemed an antiparticle that could annihilate the passive boredom invoked by television. But it also promised to surpass the book to bring about a new kind of renaissance by going beyond static representations to dynamic simulation. What kind of thinker would you become if you grew up with an active simulator connection, not just to one point of view, but to all the points of view of the ages repre-

sented so they could be dynamically tried out and compared? (quoted in Johnstone, 2003, p. 144)

Of course the argument that a new medium was cognitively stimulating had been made before, even in regard to the television programming criticized by Kay. However, the second belief underpinning the value of computers as an educational tool was unique when compared to film, radio, or television. This belief was that computers and the Internet had special value in the classroom because they had become major tools of scholarly and business activity in a way that the prior media never had. It thus became natural to want to introduce computers as tools to children in schools. As a high school teacher in one of the country's most elite private schools explained to me,

> We've been working over the years on our biology program, particularly our advanced biology program, to give students the type of experience that they need to prepare them for college work. . . . And it became obvious...over the last ten years, the computers were becoming one of the most important scientific tools available. And, so we wanted to implement the computers into the program. (Warschauer, 2000a)

CHALLENGES OF COMPUTER INTEGRATION

Computers in U.S. schools spread rapidly throughout the 1980s and 1990s, with the overall national student-computer ratio falling from 68:1 in 1983 to 6:1 in 1998 (Anderson & Ronnkvist, 1999). National and state educational policies have supported the technologization of schools in order to address challenges in teaching and learning, catalyze broader educational reform, and make the United States more economically competitive (Culp, Honey, & Mandinach, 2003). A number of scholars showcased model technology-intensive classrooms in which students became more engaged or learned better through use of computers and the Internet (e.g., see Sandholtz, 1997). Nevertheless, in most schools, computers have remained on the margins of education. Based on interviews and observations in secondary schools, Cuban (2001) claims that "less than 5 percent of teachers integrated computer technology into their regular curricular and instructional routines" and "less than 5 percent of high school students had intense 'tech-heavy' experiences" (p. 133).

In addition, unequal computer access and use in schools has been found to exacerbate social and educational divisions (e.g., see Becker,

2000b; Warschauer, 2000a; Wenglinsky, 1998). For example, Schofield and Davidson's (2004) qualitative study of Internet use in schools found that it is often provided as a privilege or reward to the most advanced students, thus amplifying already existing classroom inequality.

Finally, as pointed out by a number of critics (e.g., Healy, 1998; Oppenheimer, 2004; Stoll, 1999), computers are seldom used to promote the kind of deep learning promised by technology advocates. Oppenheimer (2004), for example, reports numerous examples of trivial or ineffective use of school computers and compares them unfavorably to his observations in a Waldorf school, where children learn through hands-on experiences with real-world objects and collaboration with each other. Though Oppenheimer's selectivity of data, sweeping conclusions, and journalistic approach have been called into question (e.g., see McKenzie's 2003 review of Oppenheimer's book), his harsh assessments have been at least partially confirmed by more rigorous studies. For example, during the 2001–02 school year, I led a team that examined technology use in 64 English, math, science, and social studies classrooms in eight diverse California high schools, based on interviews, observations, surveys, and analysis of school and classroom documents (Warschauer, Knobel, et al., 2004). While we noted a few exemplary cases of computer and Internet use by students, the overall trend was not positive, as teachers had great difficulty successfully integrating technology into the school curriculum. We characterized these difficulties in three categories, which we labeled *workability*, *complexity*, and *performativity*.

1. *Workability* referred to the degree to which the digital networks and systems in schools actually functioned for teachers and students. Many of the teachers we interviewed never came to fully trust equipment and connections that they only were able to use by occasionally bringing their class to a computer laboratory on a prearranged schedule. Teachers regularly recounted how using new technologies often doubled their workload because they had to develop a backup lesson and materials in case the network was down or the designated websites could not be accessed.
2. *Complexity* referred to the difficulty of integrating computer-based activities into instruction, even in situations where computers were readily accessible and reliable. The very need to bring students to a computer lab to achieve individual student access made such integration challenging, as computer activities could not be introduced spontaneously

at the moment of need. In addition, the fact that students had differential access to technology at home deepened the complexity. Teachers at low-SES schools were well aware that a good percentage of their students lacked computers or Internet access at home and thus might have difficulties completing computer-based homework assignments. By restricting computer use to class time, teachers often were unable to do more than cover the basics of how to use the computer program.

3. *Performativity* referred to the trend for measurable performance to become an end in itself, even in situations where it was possible to do more. In response to school and district mandates for computer literacy, teachers tended to emphasize skill at computer operations over broader learning objectives. In numerous cases, we witnessed students going through the motions of cutting and pasting material from the Internet with little cognizance of the relevance of what they were doing; in other words, online research was reduced to the skill of typing a word in a search engine and copying the first site that appeared, with insufficient attention to questions such as where to search or how to select among or evaluate located material. In other cases, we witnessed students going through the motions of PowerPoint presentations with insufficient focus on the underlying content, or even on effective communication skills with the program. For example, science students in one school we observed were given a rubric that reserved a maximal grade for students who inserted multiple fonts, sounds, slide transition types, and animations—in other words, for creating a PowerPoint presentation that distracted from rather than enhanced the underlying content.

These types of problems are broadly recognized, even by enthusiastic supporters of computers in schools. For example, few scholars in the United States have done as much to promote educational computing as Henry Becker, but his own national surveys document how only a small subset of teachers are using computers well (Becker, 2000a).

In response to these problems, some groups have mobilized against computers in schools, demanding that funding be redirected from technology to other educational expenses (e.g., see Alliance for Childhood, 2000). These arguments, however, have failed to gain traction because there appears to be broad agreement among parents, teachers, educators, and policy makers that learning with computers is of value to our children's, and our nation's, future. Instead, the trend is toward a steady increase in the amount of computer equipment in schools, based on the belief that greater access to technology will allow smoother integration into instruction (a point supported by Becker's 2000a data). Nationally, the student-computer ratio fell from 6:1 in 1998 to 3.8:1 in 2005, a decrease of nearly 40%, with schools adding not only computers but also greater Internet bandwidth and larger numbers of peripherals, such as printers, video projectors, digital whiteboards, and digital cameras (Market Data Retrieval, 2005).

Some educators argued that this wasn't enough if we were to take the tool metaphor to its logical end. If a computer is an essential tool for scholarly work, asked Seymour Papert, isn't it as necessary to provide all students with their own computer as it previously was to provide all students with their own pencil (Kyle, 2000)? Or, as Soloway (2002) asked, if business productivity picked up only after each office worker had an individual computer, wouldn't it be reasonable to assume that each student would require an individual computer before technology's promise was realized in schools? Though constrained for the time being by seemingly prohibitive costs, a movement on behalf of one-to-one computing began to coalesce.

HISTORY OF ONE-TO-ONE COMPUTING IN SCHOOLS

One-to-one computing programs in schools date back to 1990, when a private girls' school in Melbourne, Australia, started a pilot laptop program for its fifth-grade students. The program was later extended to other grade levels within the school, and over the next few years some other private schools in Australia adopted similar laptop programs. Costs for these early private-school programs were borne by parents, who either leased or purchased the laptops for their children.

A few years later Microsoft Corporation took note of the Australian programs and by 1996 was organizing conferences for educators in Washington and arranging delegations to and from Australia. By April 1997 Microsoft's initiative was officially designated as the Anytime Anywhere Learning program. Some one thousand U.S. schools participated in the program over the next 5 years, though little documentation exists as to what extent. What is clear is that most public schools had difficulty sustaining full-scale one-to-one laptop programs. In some cases, programs were attempted but not continued. In other cases, programs were limited to subgroups of students whose computers were purchased or leased by parents.

The challenge of implementing full-time one-to-one programs did not stop the expansion of laptops in schools. By 2005 fully 54% of schools had instructional laptops in their school, as compared to 43% in 2003. Laptops also rapidly increased as a percentage of total school computer inventory to 17% in 2005 from 7% in 2003. The use of laptops is supported by the growth of wireless networks, in 45% of U.S. schools in 2005 as compared to only 15% of schools in 2003 (Market Data Retrieval, 2005).

On a different note, some districts are experimenting with one-to-one desktop programs as a less expensive alternative to laptops. For example, 25 high schools in Indiana have been provided desktop computers by the state Department of Education for all students in 11th-grade English classes. The low-cost computers, which in many cases are fitted with special desks, are equipped with free or inexpensive open-source software to help guarantee the financial sustainability of the program (for pictures and information, see Indiana Department of Education, 2005). No research or evaluation studies have yet been published on the pilot program in Indiana or on other one-to-one desktop programs.

MOBILE LAPTOP CARTS

Outside of the small number of schools that have full-time laptop programs, in which all students are provided their own laptop on a daily basis, many schools make laptops available on mobile carts. These shared carts, combined with wireless networks, allow teachers to provide their students a one-to-one computing experience without having to take them to a computer laboratory. Nevertheless, mobile laptop carts clearly have several educational disadvantages when compared to full-time laptop programs. Russell, Bebell, and Higgins (2004) carried out a 2-month mixed methods study comparing use of shared laptop carts and permanent one-to-one laptops in two Massachusetts elementary schools. The laptop carts were shared among five classrooms, each of which also had three desktop computers in them. Students in the permanent one-to-one laptop program had their own laptops to use throughout the school day and at home.

Not surprisingly, the study found that students used technology a great deal more in the permanent one-to-one laptop classrooms. All uses of technology were coded by the researchers, who found that students used computers nearly seven times as much in the permanent one-to-one laptop classrooms as in the shared laptop classrooms. The differences were even more pronounced in the area of writing. Students composed text on a laptop more than 40 times as frequently in the permanent one-to-one laptop classrooms as in the shared laptop classrooms. Basically, teachers in the shared laptop classrooms continued to assign almost all their writing by hand, with students in those classrooms composing by hand eight times more frequently than on their laptops. In the permanent one-to-one laptop classroom, students wrote on laptops six times as frequently as they wrote by hand. (I will return to the issue of writing on laptops in Chapter 4.)

Homework patterns were also quite interesting. Students in the shared laptop group and the permanent one-to-one laptop group used computers at home with approximately the same frequency to download or listen to music, chat with friends, or play games. (Students in the shared laptop group used home computers for these tasks, whereas students in the one-to-one laptop group had the option of using their laptops at home.) However, students in the permanent one-to-one laptop group used computers at home much more frequently to search the Internet for class assignments or write papers for school. (I return to this issue of home-school connection of laptops in Chapter 8, analyzing data from our own study on this topic.) Finally, again not surprisingly, students in the permanent laptop group demonstrated higher levels of motivation and engagement than did students in the shared group.

At least based on this study—and nothing else has been published or reported that suggests otherwise—shared carts do not nearly match up to a full-time laptop program for achieving the educational benefits of one-to-one computing. However, shared carts are much less expensive, and thus represent an excellent transitional step for teaching and learning with laptops. Indeed, most of the schools in the present study first tried shared laptop carts before going to a full-time one-to-one program. In many cases, the use of these mobile laptop carts gave teachers and staff valuable experience in learning how to use laptops in instruction and thus smoothed the way to beginning a full-time one-to-one program.

HANDHELD COMPUTERS

As educators seek affordable ways to provide one-to-one computing options, some have advocated handheld computers. Palm Pilots and other handhelds have as much or more computing power as earlier models of desktops, and are seen by some as being highly suitable in size, durability, cost, and capacity for children's education (e.g., see British Education Communications and Technology Agency, 2004). Groups at the University of Michigan and elsewhere have developed specialized educational software to exploit the potential of handhelds for learning (see descriptions in Curtis, Williams, Norris, O'Leary, & Soloway, 2003). Two large pilot programs have been held—one in Michigan in partnership with faculty from the University of Michigan's Center for Highly Interactive Computing in Education (e.g., see Bobrowsky, Vath, Soloway, Krajcik, & Blumenfeld, 2004) and one nationally with teachers who had applied to receive sets of handhelds from the Palm Education Pioneers program (Vahey & Crawford, 2003)—and both reported positive results, including enhanced student motivation and increased collaboration and communication. Students used handhelds in these programs to brainstorm ideas with graphic organizers, copy web pages for viewing outside the class, draw and manipulate scientific models, share their work with other students and the teacher through beaming, and word process and edit their writing with the assistance of portable keyboards.

In spite of the apparent advantages of handhelds, they have not caught on in classroom instruction. In the last year for which data was available, only 4% of U.S. K–12 schools reported having any handheld computers for students. This was the same rate as the year before, indicating a stagnation of the market (Market Data Retrieval, 2004). The category of handhelds was subsequently dropped as worthy of counting and reporting in the educational technology market's flagship annual report (Market Data Retrieval, 2005), other than to list it as the lowest ranked of 18 possible technology investments by school districts. Only 1% of school districts reported in 2005 that handhelds for students represented one of their top three areas for planned technology investment, as compared to 7% that indicated digital whiteboards, 11% that indicated website upgrades, and 62% that indicated desktop or laptop computers for student use.

The limited reception that handhelds have received in schools is not really surprising. Handhelds have not done well in the overall consumer market, with many of their functions supplanted by cell phones, digital music players, or microlaptops. As for educational uses, handhelds in their current iterations lack the multimedia capability, screen size, or breadth of software that make laptops valuable for learning; and even keyboarding or accessing the Internet on a handheld involve expensive additions not ordinarily included, such as portable keyboards or wireless network cards. While some teachers have been successful in exploiting handhelds for learning, as reported above, these have almost all been highly motivated volunteers who have a strong interest in the technology. When handhelds have been distributed among teachers more broadly, the results have not been as positive, as demonstrated in the California program described next.

In this program, one of the largest pilot programs yet on handhelds in education, a school district in California distributed 1,000 Palm computers and portable keyboards to all the first-year students in two middle schools during the 2003–04 and 2004–05 school years. A total of 22 core teachers were involved in the program, including all the main subject area instructors of that grade level in the two schools. Substantial efforts and funding were put into software purchase, curriculum development, and teacher training. The program was implemented in stages, with language arts and social science emphasized in Year 1 and mathematics and science added as focus areas in Year 2.

A doctoral candidate at the University of California, Irvine, carried out observations of 40 class periods at one of the two schools as part of his dissertation research, and reported that the handhelds were used by students in only 3 of the 40 class periods (Velastegui, 2005). The school administration and staff eventually decided that the handhelds were more disruptive than beneficial to learning and collected all the handhelds from the students in the middle of Year 2, before the pilot program was even completed. At the second school, the handheld program fared better, but still not well enough to warrant schoolwide continuation beyond the 2-year pilot program. Instead, after Year 2, all teachers in the two schools and other schools in the district were invited to apply to receive a class set of the handhelds for instructional use. Only 3 of the 22 teachers in the pilot program even requested to continue using the handhelds.

Technological developments are, of course, quite fluid, and it is impossible to predict whether a new iteration of handhelds will in the future appear more attractive to schools. But presently schools are finding laptop computers a better investment for one-to-one computing, in spite of their greater expense. That view corresponds with the literacy affordances of laptops discussed in the following chapters of this book. For example, collaborative work with texts or multimedia products as students gathered around a single screen proved to be an especially powerful use of laptops, and one that would be almost impossible to replicate on a small handheld screen.

ONE-TO-ONE LAPTOP PROGRAMS

The remainder of this book will focus on what might be called complete or full-time one-to-one laptop programs, that is programs in which all the students in one or more classes in a school have individual laptop computers available throughout the school year. In most such programs, students also are allowed to take the laptops home, though in some cases the laptops must remain in school overnight. There is no reliable national data on the number of such one-to-one laptop programs in U.S. schools, but it appears from published studies (see overview in Penuel, 2005) that such programs are steadily increasing in number and size. The largest laptop program (outside of Maine) is in Henrico County, Virginia, where 14,000 high school students have been using laptops since 2001 and 11,000 middle school students have been using laptops since 2003. Pilot programs have also been started in Irving Independent School District, Texas; Broward County Public Schools, Florida; and the New Hampshire Department of Education (Bebell, 2005). I have chosen in this book to examine laptop programs in two states, California and Maine, which, between them, represent a diverse sample of laptop programs in the United States.

Maine's Statewide Laptop Program

The flagship U.S. laptop program is in Maine, where the state Department of Education has provided laptop computers to all seventh-grade students since fall 2002 and all eighth-grade students since fall 2003. In 2004, the program was extended to high schools, though on a voluntary basis, with individual districts and schools assuming the costs. A total of 31 of the state's 176 high schools joined during the 2004–05 school year, and new state financial incentives seek to bring more high schools into the program.

Maine adopted the laptop program at a time when its school test scores were already among the highest in the nation, but when it was struggling to remain economically competitive as some of its core industries, such as logging, were suffering. The rationale behind the Maine program is worth quoting at length because it represents how the past-to-future metaphor shapes the United States's largest laptop program. The statement served as the introduction to the report of a prestigious statewide task force assembled by the government on behalf of the laptop program:

> We live in a world that is increasingly complex and where change is
> increasingly rampant. Driving much of this complexity and change are

new concepts and a new economy based on powerful, ubiquitous computer technology linked to the Internet.

Twenty years ago, personal computers were a relative novelty. Today, two thirds of Maine workers use computers in their workplace. Ten years ago, the Internet as we know it did not exist; today, it drives communication, information, entertainment, and the fortunes of stock market portfolios. From the complex to the mundane, in a thousand small and sometimes unnoticed ways, computer technology has permeated our economy and changed our daily lives. Some uses of electronic technology are so ubiquitous they are unnoticed—nearly all of us use ATM machines for routine banking transactions, for example. Many newsletters and bulletins are already beginning to transition to electronic-only distribution. Increasingly, examinations for graduate schools and for various professional licensing requirements are on-line —some exclusively on-line. The technological transformation is not limited to "high-tech" businesses; main-line manufacturing, farming, service and retail industries are increasingly harnessing computer technology to improve processes, boost productivity, and innovate new approaches to stay competitive.

Our schools are challenged to prepare young people to navigate and prosper in this world, with technology as an ally rather than an obstacle. The challenge is familiar, but the imperative is new: we must prepare young people to thrive in a world that doesn't exist yet, to grapple with problems and construct new knowledge which is barely visible to us today. It is no longer adequate to prepare some of our young people to high levels of learning and technological literacy; we must prepare *all* for the demands of a world in which workers and citizens will be required to use and create knowledge, and embrace technology as a powerful tool to do so.

If technology is a challenge for our educational system, it is also part of the solution. To move all students to high levels of learning and technological literacy, *all* students will need access to technology when and where it can be most effectively incorporated into learning. With the guidance of good teachers with technological facility, computer technology and the Internet can provide students with a pipeline to explore real world concepts, interact with real world experts, and analyze and solve real world problems. Computers and the Internet offer the potential to keep classroom resources and materials current with the contemporary world to an extent that is unprecedented. Computer technology also offers opportunities for self-directed, personalized learning projects that can tailor the curriculum to student interests and engagement, and allow teachers to facilitate active student learning rather than merely the rote transfer of information. (Task Force on the Maine Learning Technology Endowment, 2001, p. i)

The implementation of the program in Maine corresponded to these goals, as well as to the state's progressive educational traditions. A statewide group within the Department of Education, the Maine Learning Technology Initiative (MLTI), was assembled to lead the effort. Apple was chosen as the vendor with the belief that its operating system and software products would facilitate the creativity, communication, and media production the program sought to foster. Considerable resources were put into curriculum development, teacher professional development, and teacher networking. An MLTI teacher leader was appointed at every school and regular meetings were scheduled in school districts and regions to foster subject-specific teacher learning or exchange of ideas. Project-based learning was strongly promoted within teacher professional development events and further reinforced through articles and resources posted on the MLTI website.

In spite of the ambitious nature of the Maine laptop project, almost no peer-reviewed research has yet been published about it, other than a brief article from our own research team (Warschauer, Grant, Del Real, & Rousseau, 2004) reporting on laptops and academic literacy development among English language learners. (Evaluation reports have been issued by the Center for Education Policy, 2005; Davies, 2004; and the Great Maine Schools Project, 2004.) The analysis of laptop learning in Maine in this book thus represents one of the first published discussions of independent research on the project.

Laptop Programs in California

California, in many ways, represents the polar opposite of Maine. While Maine is a small rural state, trying to remain economically relevant, California is the most heavily populated state in the country and a global economic power. While Maine is 99% White and English-speaking, California is a majority-minority state at the forefront of new immigration patterns. While Maine has well-funded schools with small class sizes, high test scores, and a history of progressive education, California has poorly funded schools with large class sizes, low test scores, and a penchant for strictly controlled basics-style education. California has not implemented a statewide laptop program, nor does there seem any possibility it will do so in the near future, given economic realities in the state. However, as in other states, numerous individual schools and districts are adopting laptop programs. These programs thus provide an opportunity to study laptop learning in a very different context from that of Maine.

Laptop programs have existed in public schools in California since 1996, when representatives of Clovis Unified School District near

Fresno participated in the original Microsoft Anytime Anywhere Learning program. Since that time, individual laptop programs have ebbed and flowed, as schools and districts have faced the financial challenges of maintaining the programs, but overall the number of programs has gradually increased, especially in the main urban and suburban areas of the Bay Area and Southern California. Research in this book has focused on Orange County and adjacent areas of southern Los Angeles County, together a racially and ethnically diverse metropolitan area encompassing some 4 million people. Here the number of full-time laptop programs—defined as those programs in which one or more classes of students had full-time access to laptops every day of the school year—expanded from five schools in 2003–04 to eight schools in 2005–06.

Laptop programs in California are funded from a combination of three sources: grants, parents, and school districts. Grants are provided either by the technology industry, foundations, or the federal government to provide better technology integration in schools. Grant funding has proven to be the least stable way of supporting a laptop program, as grants inevitably run out. However, grant funding is useful for launching pilot programs, which can then be built upon through other funding models. For example, the largest districtwide one-to-one laptop program in Southern California was preceded by a federal grant for a mobile laptop pilot program, the success of which was used as a basis for launching the full-time one-to-one program with district and parent funding.

Many laptop programs in California have come to rely on some type of parental support. Typically, a volunteer laptop program is established and parents are requested to purchase or lease a laptop for their child to participate in the program. Children in the laptop program take one or more of their classes in special laptop classes. Children who don't have laptops take regular courses that supposedly follow the same curriculum, but without laptops. Such parent-funded programs are the most sustainable, since they don't rely on district funding for purchase of hardware or software, but they are limited in terms of the numbers of students they can reach, and highly problematic in terms of educational equity. Therefore, a number of schools have attempted to combine parental funding with district funding. In these jointly funded programs, parents are still urged to purchase or lease laptops for their children, but the school district puts in additional funding (either from its regular budget or from federal programs for high-poverty schools) to support the participation of children who could not otherwise participate. In some cases, these funds might be used to pay part of the lease fee for low-income families. In other cases, funds are used to purchase additional school-owned laptops that are then lent to low-income students who participate.

The motivations behind laptop programs in California vary. In most cases, they are similar to those in Maine, with the proponents in particular school districts feeling strongly that laptop programs are highly beneficial for achieving the type of schooling necessary in the twenty-first century. In other cases, motivations are influenced by issues of equality, based on the belief that minority or limited-English-speaking students need school access to computers to make up for lack of home access or other educational disadvantages.

RESEARCH ON ONE-TO-ONE LAPTOP PROGRAMS

The largest educational laptop studies to date are an evaluation of the laptop program in eight schools in Microsoft's Anytime Anywhere Learning project (Walker, Rockman, & Chessler, 2000) and a statewide study of the Maine laptop program (Silvernail & Lane, 2004). Both of these studies appear to be commissioned evaluation reports (the former by Microsoft and the latter by the Maine Department of Education) and both rely principally on surveys and interviews to document how laptops were used. The conclusions of the two studies are similar in pointing to an increased amount of technology use following implementation of laptop programs, positive attitudes toward the programs by students and teachers, more autonomous learning, and a high degree of student engagement. Neither study systematically incorporated observations into their methodology.

In addition to these 2 larger scale studies, some 30 smaller researcher studies on learning with laptops were published between 2001 and 2005 (for a listing and review, see Penuel, 2005). Overall, the research suggests that "students use laptops primarily for writing, taking notes, completing homework assignments, keeping organized, communicating with peers and their teachers, and researching topics on the Internet. . . .These students who do engage in more extended projects typically use design and multimedia tools, including presentation software and software for making and editing digital images and movies" (p. 3–4). The implementation of laptop programs, as with other uses of technology, is highly shaped by teachers' attitudes (see in particular Windschitl & Sahl, 2002), and professional development is thus critical for successful implementation, as is sufficient technical support.

There is little in this corpus of research to suggest that use of laptops results in improved tests scores. The Anytime Anywhere Learning study (Walker et al., 2000) attempted to look at learning outcomes by drawing comparisons to similar schools or to prior cohorts at the same schools, but was not able to demonstrate any substantive test score gains. Similarly, test scores in Maine have remained flat following the initial 2-year implementation of the programs. Some of the smaller studies have concluded improved outcomes in writing, but the conclusions are questionable due to the methodology of the studies (see Penuel, 2005). In any case, Maine remains the largest laboratory so far, and writing test scores have not improved there statewide. In all of these studies, the only measurable student outcome that has been shown to improve is technological proficiency (see Penuel, 2005; Schaumburg, 2001).

The failure of laptop programs to raise test scores has been attributed to a number of factors, including an insensitivity of current tests to the types of twenty-first-century learning that laptops are trying to promote (see Silvernail, 2005; Walker et al., 2000). Silvernail, for example, compares the rather restrictive types of problem solving that are required for the Maine Educational Assessment to the broader types of analysis that are put forth as demonstrating twenty-first-century learning skills, and suggests they are quite different. There is certainly little on standardized tests to assess students' ability to rapidly find, critique, analyze, and deploy new information, nor are there items that test students' ability to interpret or produce multimedia, including images, sounds, video, animation, and texts. Even writing, which should be the measurable skill most amenable to improvement through laptop programs, is problematic to assess, since the paper-and-pencil assessments of standardized tests are known to substantially underestimate the writing ability of students who have learned to write on computers (see Russell & Plati, 2002). The relationship of standardized test scores and learning with laptops will be discussed in more detail in the following two chapters.

In summary, though school laptop programs are growing in number, there have been relatively few independent, peer-reviewed studies of these programs, and fewer still that have looked beyond one or two schools. No prior studies have carried out extensive and systematic observations of laptop programs in a number of schools, nor have prior studies focused on culturally and linguistically diverse learners, including large numbers of English language learners. And no prior study has used the lens of literacy as its focus, combining an analysis of "traditional" literacies, such as reading and writing, with "new" literacies, such as information literacy and media design.

THE LAPTOPS AND LITERACY STUDY

Much of the rest of this book will draw on data from a 2-year laptop and literacy study conducted at the University of California, Irvine (UCI), from 2003–2005. I was joined in this research by 10 graduate and undergraduate students at UCI and a colleague from Southern Methodist University (see the Acknowledgments). Most of the other participating researchers focused on a couple of schools and examined particular issues of interest to them (e.g., laptops and literacy in upper elementary grades, academic literacy in high school laptop programs, automated essay scoring in the laptop classroom). I participated in the research at all the schools in the study and maintained the overall general focus on laptops and literacy. The overall research design was that of the multisite case study, an approach I have often used previously (e.g., see Warschauer, 1999; Warschauer, 2000a; Warschauer, Knobel, et al., 2004). Case study research allows intensive examination of particular cases, thus helping address the *how* and *why* questions that are best answered by close-up investigation. Then, by combining a number of different cases in a particular multisite study, a researcher can step back from the individual cases and try to draw general conclusions.

The Schools

In order to capture the diversity of laptop programs in the United States, 10 schools in two very different states, California and Maine, were chosen (see Table 2.1). A purposefully stratified sample of schools was chosen to get as broad a representation of laptop programs as possible. The sample includes 2 elementary schools, 4 middle or junior high schools, 3 high schools, and 1 combined elementary-junior high. Students in these schools use laptops in grades ranging from third to twelfth. The schools are located in urban, suburban, and rural settings, and are located in upper-class, middle-class, and poor neighborhoods. The ethnic composition of the schools varies widely, with Whites, Latinos, Asians and Asian Americans, and African Americans each forming the largest ethnic group in at least one school. Most of the schools in the study have integrated laptops into their general school programs, but in certain schools the laptops are principally or exclusively used in

Table 2.1. School Sites in Laptop and Literacy Study, 2003–2005

School	Grades of Laptop Program	Location	Principal Ethnic Groups	SES	Program	Funding	Platform
Henry Elementary	3–6	Suburban California	White, Asian	Medium	Gifted	Parental lease	Macintosh
Flower School	3–7	Suburban California	Asian, White	High	General	Parental lease	Macintosh
River Elementary	4	Urban California	Latino	Low	Language arts/ESL	Private grant	Windows
Nancy Jr. High	7	Urban California	Latino, White	Low	General	Federal	Macintosh
Howard Middle	7–8	Suburban Maine	White	High	General	State	Macintosh
Castle Middle	7–8	Urban Maine	White, Black	Low	General	State	Macintosh
Freedom Middle	8	Urban California	Black, Latino	Low	Alternative/at-risk	Private grant	Macintosh
Carlton High	9–12	Urban California	Asian, White	High	Academic core	Parental purchase	Windows & Macintosh
Melville High	9–12	Suburban California	White, Latino	High	Academic core	Parental purchase	Windows
Plum High	9–12	Rural Maine	White	Low	General	State and private	Macintosh

Note: All names are pseudonyms. In a previous article (Warschauer et al., 2004a), River Elementary and Castle Middle were referred to as Adelante and Urbania, respectively.

special programs, such as those for at-risk or gifted students. Funding for the laptop programs is provided from a variety of federal, state, and private sources, including in some cases parental purchase or lease, and the platforms deployed include Windows, Macintosh, or, in one school, both.

The Data

Data collection at the schools involved a combination of observations, interviews, surveys, and document review. In 6 of the 10 schools, a team of researchers visited the school part of the day one or two times per week for most of a school year to conduct the research. In the remaining 4 schools, the research was compacted, with a team of researchers visiting the school all day for 4–5 days straight. At all the schools, the administration allowed us to observe and interview whomever we wished, but participation by any individual teacher, parent, or student was voluntary. Five to seven individual case study students were chosen at each school to represent the diversity of students at the school (by grade level, language background, gender, ethnicity, and whether they were high or low achievers).

A total of 650 hours of classroom observations were conducted at the 10 schools, with detailed field notes taken during all observations. Interviews were conducted with 61 teachers, 32 other school staff (administrators, librarians, counselors, or technology coordinators), 67 students, and 31 parents. Interviews ranged from 20 to 60 minutes, and a number of the people were interviewed multiple times. All interviews were tape-recorded and transcribed.

Teachers and students in 3 of the 10 schools completed a voluntary anonymous online survey with a response rate of 100% for the teachers (35 out of 35) and 86% for the students (877 out of 1,012). We also collected documents and records from individual schools, including school, district, and state policy documents; print and digital teaching materials; print and digital assignments completed by case study students; and, in some cases, school or student test score or attendance records.

Data was analyzed through standard qualitative methods, first to identify key patterns within each research site, and then to make comparisons and find commonalities or differences across research sites. To assist this analysis, all the interviews and field notes were coded using the HyperResearch software program (ResearchWare, 2005) using a bottom-up coding scheme that considered whatever items of interest emerged from the data related to the overall theme of literacy and learning with laptops. A total of 381 separate codes were generated (e.g., reading—background information, writing—revising, information—evaluating online material, media—content vs. look, problems—distraction), and 3,397 instances of these codes were marked.

A discussion of this data in relation to literacy forms the bulk of this book, beginning with the "traditional" literacies of reading and writing.

CHAPTER 3

Reading

I have a lot of reluctant readers, which is where the laptops come in really handy in reading class because the kids love them. I've found that I can get them to read what they're interested in online without them even knowing that they're reading. If I asked them to pick up a book, I won't hear the end of it of how terrible it is. For instance today, we're learning about nonfiction and the different tools that nonfiction uses to help you learn, such as diagrams, captions, pictures. They're making a slideshow of each tool that you can use. So today they were doing diagrams and labeling things and these two boys decided to diagram a snake and they spent 20 minutes reading about a snake online and in a book. If I'd asked them to read about snakes, there's no way they would have.

—Reading specialist teacher, Castle Middle School

Reading is rightly viewed as the cornerstone of academic literacy and education. It is also an area in which U.S. education is doing poorly. The percentage of 17-year-old students in the United States who are able to read and understand complicated information was actually lower in 2004 than in 1971, the first year for which comparable data is available (National Center for Educational Statistics, 2005). In other words, at the very age when youth are getting ready to graduate high school and enter higher education or the work force, they cannot even read as well as youth of three decades ago, at the very beginning of the information revolution.

Paradoxically, though, reading scores at certain grade and skill levels are improving. In particular, the percentage of 9-year-olds with basic reading abilities has improved (National Center for Educational Statistics, 2005). We are doing a better job than previously in helping our third graders decode simple texts, but this is not translating into improved comprehension among our high school students.

This paradox is explained in part by the nature of educational reform in reading, which has placed overwhelming focus on promoting those decoding skills that will allow short-term gain in basic reading proficiencies for young children, while shortchanging the meaning-making skills and enculturation into academic literacy that will lead to higher proficiencies as children get older. Scholars have known for decades (e.g., see Flesch, 1955), that phonemic awareness (the understanding that oral words are composed of individual sounds) and knowledge of phonics (matching letters to sounds) are critical components of early reading skills. A sharpened focus on phonemic awareness and phonics is one reason that early reading skills have improved in the United States. However, like many educational reform movements, a grain of truth became oversimplified in an ideological battleground and was turned into a weapon against other elements of truth. In this case, though phonics is a valuable component of reading instruction, it is far from being the only important component; in fact, it is of any real value only at the very early stages of reading instruction. Yet phonics has been actively promoted in the United States not as part of a meaning-making process but in opposition to an emphasis on meaning making.

This one-sided view of reading has contributed to a major educational problem known as the *fourth-grade slump* (Chall, Jacobs, & Baldwin, 1990). This term describes a well-documented phenomenon in which reading scores of low-SES students drop precipitously from the fourth grade on. This contributes both to the overall lowering of reading test scores in the United States for middle and high school students as well as the vast disparity on reading tests and other educational outcome measures by SES and race.

The fourth grade represents a critical turning point for learning because it is at that level that children must make a transition from *learning to read* to *reading to learn* (Chall, 1996). In the early elementary grades, children practice decoding and understanding extremely simple texts made up of basic language from everyday life. By the upper elementary grades, though, children must learn to comprehend more challenging texts involving complex language from a wide range of decontextualized settings. The sample third- and fifth-grade texts included in Figure 3.1 from the widely adopted *Open Court Reading* series (McGraw Hill, 2005a, 2005b) illustrate the transition that readers go through in fourth grade, with some of the key words in each text italicized. The third-grade text is about an event that children might often see in front of their own houses, and emphasizes everyday vocabulary. The fifth-grade text discusses a scientific event far removed from children's physical experience and includes abstract vocabulary not used by children in their daily life.

ACADEMIC LANGUAGE PROFICIENCY

Two overlapping sets of resources are critical toward understanding these more sophisticated upper elementary texts, and both of these are distributed highly unequally by SES in the United States: academic language proficiency and cultural capital. Academic language proficiency refers to knowledge of the specialized vocabulary and syntax of academic texts and communication. All children learn the basic vocabulary that they need for everyday life (e.g., *house, chair, table*), but only a subset of children learn the more specialized vocabulary featured in academic texts (e.g., *override, grasp, lunar*). Learning these more complex vocabulary items in early childhood is highly dependent on hearing and using them at home, and the quantity and quality of vocabulary that children are exposed to has been shown to be dramatically unequal; one study suggests that the children of professional parents hear an estimated 30 million more words than the children of families receiving public assistance by the time they reach the age of 3 (Hart & Risley, 1995). In addition, middle-class and high-SES children are much more likely to gain exposure to the kinds of complex syntax used in academic language, such as embedded clauses or passive tense, because their parents more frequently draw them into analytic discussion (Heath, 1983). These analytic discussions also serve to enculturate middle- and upper-middle-class children into the kinds of decontextualized thinking that is an essential component of comprehending academic texts.

CULTURAL CAPITAL

The last point overlaps with the issue of cultural capital, which refers to the cultural background, knowledge base, skills, and attitudes that families transmit to their children (Bourdieu, 1986). A critical element of cultural capital in relationship to reading is *background knowledge*. Almost all children in elementary school are familiar with the everyday topics, such as moving vans loading furniture, that are prominent in Grades 1–3 reading. However, only a subset of children have knowledge about the broad array of topics from the sciences, social studies, and arts that become more dominant in Grades 4–6 reading. And when you don't have a background in a topic, it makes it much harder to guess unfamiliar vocabulary, understand complex syntax, or derive meaning from a passage.

Figure 3.1. Sample Third- and Fifth-Grade Text Passages

Third-Grade Text	Fifth-Grade Text
A block from our *house* I *saw* a moving *van* in front of a *brown house*, and men were *carrying* in *chairs* and *tables* and *bookcases* and *boxes* full of I don't know what.	Armstrong *grasped* the *rocket control handle* with his right hand and *overrode* the *automatic landing system*. Eagle *skimmed* over the large field of boulders as Armstrong searched the *lunar surface* for a smoother landing area.
(Text from *Open Court Reading, Level 3*, McGraw Hill, 2005a, p. 15, italics added.)	(Text from *Open Court Reading, Level 5*, McGraw Hill, 2005b, p. 554, italics added.)

Beyond background knowledge are the general attitudes and sense of identity that children grow up with. Gee (2004) makes a compelling argument that reading is, to a large extent, learned not as a natural process (like learning to speak or walk) or an instructed process (like learning arithmetic), but rather as a cultural process (like learning to cook or to hunt). Middle-class children learn to read because they have grown up in print-rich environments where reading is valued, they see their family members reading, and they are exposed (through conversation, travel, visits to museums, and so on) to the kinds of topics that are featured in school texts. They thus grow up with a disposition to read and with the relevant background knowledge to succeed at it.

Reading can be taught through an instructed process, which accounts for the fact that most children master phonics in early grades and thus do well on early reading test scores. But, as Gee argues, those who learn primarily through an instructed process are at a distinct disadvantage when they get to upper grades because they have neither the background knowledge nor disposition to tackle complex, decontextualized texts on a broad range of topics. Thus they begin to fail at reading and, in response to failing, become increasingly disengaged from school. The downward spiral of failure, disengagement, and further failure often continues through high school and beyond. In California, for example, more than 40% of African American and Latino students fail to graduate (Orfield, Losen, Wald, & Swanson, 2004), and of those who remain in school by the end of 11th grade, only 21% of each group achieve proficient levels in their state English language arts test. This represents a strong drop-off from the 4th grade, when 35% of African Americans and 32% of Latinos achieve proficiency in English language arts.

ADDRESSING THE GAP

What does this mean for teaching and learning reading in school? Schools need to seriously address the gaps in academic language proficiency and cultural capital that lead to reading failure. From upper elementary grades on, four steps have been identified as critical to supporting improved reading, especially by culturally and linguistically diverse students from low-SES backgrounds:

1. Extensive reading of large amounts of increasingly challenging material can help provide students the exposure to academic language, and in particular to large amounts of vocabulary, that they will need to continue improving (Krashen, 2004).
2. Intensive work with language, involving focused analysis of words, sentences, and texts, can help improve students' academic language proficiency and give them a better understanding of how academic texts are produced and interpreted (Cummins, 2005).
3. Provision of sufficient background knowledge can provide scaffolding so that students can succeed at increasingly complex reading tasks (Christen & Murphy, 1991).
4. Involvement of students in activities that are cognitively, emotionally, and behaviorally engaging and that promote their identity as readers, writers, and learners can help acculturate students into a positive reading environment (Guthrie, 2004).

Prior research suggests that certain uses of technology can further these goals but others do not. Probably the best known and most ambitious use of technology for reading is via integrated learning systems that provide carefully orchestrated drill and practice. Such programs do offer intensive work with language, but in a context that tends to disengage rather than fully engage students. Kulik (2003) recently reviewed 27 studies of technology use in K–12 learning programs, including 9 studies of integrated learning systems, and found no evidence of a positive contribution of integrated learning systems to reading (for one recent study on the matter, see Paterson, Henry, O'Quin, & Ceptrano, 2003).

Kulik's meta-analysis did indicate modest positive benefits for two technology-based interventions on reading: writing-to-read programs and extensive reading management programs. Writing-to-read programs involve emergent readers writing words, sentences, or stories of interest and then learning to read them. These programs are exclusively used in lower elementary grades and were thus not a factor in the current laptop study.

Reading management programs, such as Accelerated Reader (Renaissance Learning, 2004) and Reading Counts (Scholastic, 2004), are used to encourage extensive reading through better management of free-time voluntary reading programs. Students first take a reading test to determine their level, and then the programs recommend a large number of books appropriate to that level. Students then check out recommended books from the school library, read them, and then take a brief quiz online to confirm that the book has been read and comprehended. If the student passes the quiz, further books are recommended at that level and eventually at higher levels as the student proceeds through the program. Several of the laptop schools in the study used these reading management programs.

THE CALIFORNIA SCHOOLS

The provision of one-to-one laptops allows schools and teachers much greater leeway to promote reading via technology, and most of the schools we observed did so, in line with the four instructional strategies mentioned above. In particular, almost all schools attempted to use laptops to create a much more engaging reading environment for students and thus promote their identities as readers, writers, and learners. How this was accomplished will be illustrated through discussion of individual laptop programs in California at the elementary, junior high, and high school levels.

River Elementary: Mr. Molina's Fourth Grade

River Elementary School is located in a low-income Latino community within a racially diverse city of Southern California. Some 98% of the students in the school are Latino, 97% are low-income, and 73% are classified as English-language learners. As a Grades 4–6 school in a struggling immigrant neighborhood, River Elementary daily confronts the challenges of upper elementary school outlined above. And it does so pretty well. Though test scores are low—the typical River student reads 2 years below grade level—they are higher than those for most other demographically similar schools across the state. River also has an excellent learning environment, with a serious atmosphere, a respectful student population, and a well-qualified teaching staff; 97% of the school's teachers have full teaching credentials compared to the state average of only 91%.

Much of River's success is due to its energetic principal, Mr. Karl, who had been with the school since its founding 7 years previous to our study there. Mr. Karl is deeply devoted to helping at-risk students achieve educational equity and is a strong proponent of the potential of technology for assisting this aim. The school has a strong focus on reading, the centerpiece of which is the Accelerated Reader software program (Renaissance Learning, 2004) for extensive reading management. Mr. Karl and his staff have assembled in the school library more than 16,000 books for which Accelerated Reader computerized quizzes are available, and all teachers in the school are expected to devote time and energy to what is referred to as "sustained silent reading" using these books. Children at the school check out, and are quizzed upon, approximately one book per day per student, and River has achieved the rank of "master school" within the Renaissance Learning program (the equivalent of a black belt in reading promotion).

The emphasis on reading and technology extends to many other aspects of the school. Students spend nearly half the school day (2.5 hours) in a special class, organized by language and reading level, called English Language Arts, in which reading and language development are the principal foci. For the last several years, the school has also had a steadily expanding Technology Academy, with all teachers in the academy having access to digital whiteboards in their classrooms and shared laptop carts. Following the success of the academy, the school's principal, vice-principal, and technology coordinator put together a grant proposal to a foundation for a pilot one-to-one laptop program in one of its English Language Arts classes. The grant was funded, and a class set of Toshiba laptop computers were delivered to the school in time for the 2003–04 school year. Mr. Molina, a young, highly effective teacher and technology enthusiast, was tapped to make use of the laptops in his fourth-grade language arts class.

Though Mr. Molina's class was one of the higher level language arts groups in the school, the average reading level was still one year below grade level. A total of 27 of the 28 students in the class were Latino, and the majority of them were classified as English-language learners, at a variety of levels. Though we observed the program during the first year of implementation, Mr. Molina had had substantial prior experience teaching with shared laptop carts, and he and the class adjusted very quickly. The demographics of the school, the talent of the teacher, and the full support from the administration all came together to allow a fascinating look at the use of technology to help at-risk students bump over the fourth-grade slump.

Mr. Molina, previously honored as the school's teacher of the year, did not disappoint. He masterfully and almost seamlessly integrated the laptops into instruction in a way that supported his ambitious instructional objectives. For Molina, the laptops became part of a broad array of teaching resources, including a digital whiteboard, wireless network, some digital cameras, a few desktop computers, a printer, the classroom walls, and the school library, all of which were orchestrated together in a harmonious and engaging learning environment. This is illustrated by examining the types of technology-enhanced activities that take place to prepare students for reading; to support independent reading; and to help students analyze, interpret and extend what they had read.

Like most of the laptop classes we visited, Molina's room was a print-rich environment. Student work filled the walls, along with a wide array of instructional material. Molina made frequent use of his own laptop and the digital whiteboard to call up background information to better motivate and inform students' reading. This included posters, pictures, maps, and texts related to the stories they were about to read or to the authors of those stories. These materials often served as a basis for class discussion, and vice versa; if students had questions as Molina was introducing a story, he quickly and readily brought up additional information on the topic from the Internet.

Molina also regularly sent the students on information-seeking activities known as WebQuests (Dodge, 2005) in preparation for reading. For example, before they read a story on wildfires they performed a WebQuest on the topic that required searching for information on the Internet about what wildfires are, which environmental and meteorological factors contribute to them, and how they are fought. In assigning these WebQuests, Molina had a dual purpose: both providing background knowledge for upcoming assignments and simultaneously developing different kinds of reading skills and strategies. He explained the different reading skills:

> Reading on the Internet is a completely different type of reading than the reading from a storybook. They're having to navigate Web pages, filter out some of the superfluous information that Web pages have, and then pare it down to where the information is.

Students also used their computers for vocabulary activities prior to reading. The use of computers allowed additional learning resources to be brought to this task, such as picture-vocabulary matching exercises, as well as the creation of a more visible, collaborative learning environment, with students working together at each other's screens or sharing their work at the digital whiteboard.

The support for independent reading took place largely through the Accelerated Reader program. Though this did not involve the laptops per se, it is worth briefly mentioning as an example of how Molina wove various technologies and resources into an effective instructional program. Molina took a highly engaged approach to Accelerated Reader, suggesting titles to students, meeting with students individually to discuss what they had read, and having them fill out special strategy cards for their reading that indicated, for example, what predictions they made as they were reading and how those predictions turned out. He also created a highly celebratory environment of students' independent reading accomplishments, through wall charts, awards ceremonies, and other forms of encouraging independent reading.

The most extensive use of laptops was in after-reading activities. Molina's students used laptops to analyze the texts they had read and to extend their thinking about those texts in multiple ways. Text analysis occurred in multiple ways. Students made use of graphic organizing or spreadsheet software to make outlines of the genre, main ideas, timeline, or content of stories they had read. For example, after reading a story on wildfires, students made use of graphic organizing software to outline the role that wildfires play in the lifecycle of forests. Through the software the students were able to organize quotations into bubbles of text that were arranged in the shape of a cycle. In addition to locating appropriate quotes from the text, the students copied and pasted pictures from clip art and the Internet that illustrated the main idea of each quote. This required students to reread the text to locate and clarify key points, while organizing their understanding of the text into a visual representation. In order to search for images in clip art or the Internet, the students were forced to articulate their understanding of the text in a one- or two-word summary, which provided further need to think about the meaning of the story and express key concepts in one or two keywords.

In another example, students used graphic organizing software to map out the organizational components of a story, PowerPoint to put together a presentation on the main idea of a story, and tables or spreadsheets to chart information about timeline or character development. In none of these examples was technology required; in all of them, the teacher found it helpful. This was not only because students were enthusiastic about using the technology—enthusiasm that in some cases may wear off with time—but also because technological elements helped organize students' thinking. These included the visual elements, which helped make certain features and relationships more salient (through use of different shapes, colors, arrows, and so on), as well as the malleability features, with students able to easily revise or add to whatever they created or copy it and reuse it in another analysis. Such digitized work also was much more readable than handwritten work and thus susceptible to collaborative review, whether in small groups at students' desks or via presentation on the digital whiteboard to the whole class.

Many of the after-reading tasks in Molina's class were used to strengthen the reading-writing connection. For example, after mapping out the main elements of a story they read, as discussed above, students then used the same graphic organizing template to plan their own writing. We observed two other interesting examples of the reading-writing connection after students read *Sadako and the Thousand Paper Cranes* by Eleanor Coerr (1999). First, students honed their ability to read and follow written instructions by making their own paper cranes according to directions the class had found online. They then designed their original origami, wrote out instructions on how to make them, and took digital pictures of themselves to illustrate the instructions. The class collectively edited the instructions, printed them out together with the photos, and assembled them into a class origami book. The activity was highly engaging and it allowed the students to immerse themselves in the experience of making paper cranes and other origami, as had the Japanese children in Coerr's book. More important, though, the activity also helped the students focus on instructional vocabulary and syntax (e.g., "crease sharply and unfold back to a square") that helped stretch their academic language proficiency.

Following this, the students engaged in an online book-review activity. The class went to Amazon.com, and collectively critiqued some of the customer reviews of *Sadako and the Thousand Paper Cranes*. In doing so, they discussed the particular features of an effective book review, such as how to provide an attention-getting title, how to gain readers' interest, and how to avoid giving away too much through "spoilers." In examining published customer reviews, the students also took careful note of grammatical or spelling errors and reinforced their own commitment to do better. Students then wrote their own reviews of *Sadako and the Thousand Paper Cranes* and saved them on the school file server. Molina then made suggestions to the students through the use of the comment feature in Microsoft Word, and students retrieved their files and revised their reviews. The students then submitted their reviews for publication on Amazon.com and checked back with great delight a couple of days later to see that they had been published. Through the activity, the students learned not only to think more about the book they had read, but also to become more thoughtful readers of book reviews, by studying the online book review genre and even writing and publishing their own reviews. Notice, for example, in the review by Elena, a 10-year-old student from Mexico, how she tries to grab the reader's attention with a bold headline and then reveals just enough of the plot to keep readers interested without providing the details of the sad ending (see Figure 3.2).

Nancy Junior High: Ms. Patterson's Classes

Nancy Junior High is located about a half-hour drive from River Elementary. Its students, also predominately Latino, face even greater challenges than those of the students at River Elementary. By the time low-income Latino students in California reach junior high, many have progressed from a fourth-grade slump to what is termed the *eighth-grade cliff*, following several years of declining test scores and increasing disengagement from school. At the same time, immigrants who arrive in the United States at a later age also face serious obstacles, with relatively few years to catch up with English language and literacy skills before the age of high school graduation.

Ms. Patterson, a language arts and ESL teacher at Nancy, teaches both of these types of Latino students—those who have been in the school system since kindergarten and those who have immigrated more recently. The former are largely in her regular English language arts classes and the latter in her ESL classes. We observed her teaching both types of classes on a regular basis. The use of laptops in these classes was similar in broad strokes to that of Mr. Molina's class, with students using their computers and the Internet to engage in language analysis, gather background information, and analyze and extend texts they had read. As did Molina, Patterson made use of computers and the Internet to help students gain access to a world of literature that otherwise may have been excessively challenging to them. Patterson discussed how she used the Internet to help open up students' understanding of texts:

> We read a short poem by Emily Dickinson ["I'm nobody! Who are you"] and they just weren't getting what she was saying in the poem and so we were able to do a quick little search online and they were able to see pictures of her and her dad. And they read about how she lost her father and how she sort of lived this strange isolated life and then I think they grasped the poem.

Figure 3.2. Student Book Review on Amazon.com

★★★★★ **Huge Hit!!**, May 6, 2004

A Kid's Review

Sadako and the Thousand Paper Cranes is a great story it's about a brave young girl. The story takes place in Hiroshima, Japan when the atom bomb was dropped. This story is so sad, that when I read it my eyes were filled with tears. If you go to Hiroshima there might be a lot of reminders of her. So I recommend you to get this book. The ending of this story is so, so sad that it will put tears in your eyes.

In a similar example, students had to write an interpretation of "The Highwayman," a poem by Alfred Noyes. To help the students get through the material, Patterson brought the students to a website, where the poem was accompanied by photographs and artwork that helped illustrate the story. They also went online to get information on material discussed in the poem, such as Napoleonic cocked hats, which further helped clarify the story for them.

Perhaps the most interesting example to us, and one that we observed over several class sessions, was the use of the Internet to support students' understanding of *Beowulf*, an epic poem that is considered the earliest existing piece of writing from Old English. The original poem describes the tale of the heroic warrior, Beowulf, who helps bring his people in southern Sweden 50 years of peace. Though the poem was read in a modernized narrative version (Nye, 1968), the context, language, and genre of the 100-page adaptation were all sufficiently foreign to students to make the poem quite a challenge for this group of at-risk seventh-grade students. Yet as other students in California, they were expected to read, understand, and interpret it.

Before reading *Beowulf*, Patterson's students first went online to gather background information about the author, the story, and the conditions of medieval life. Using teacher-suggested websites, they answered questions such as "What language was *Beowulf* written in?" "What's an epic?" "Where and when did the story come from?" "What qualities do knights aspire to?" and "What did young people do during medieval times?"

While reading the story, they consulted a website (Driver, 2000) that included a multimedia narrative account of parts of the story. This allowed them to draw on imagery to support language. It also allowed them to contrast two alternate tellings of the same story. After completing the story, they pursued the theme of alternate tellings further by writing a summation of what occurred in *Beowulf* from the point of view of a particular character.

The most animated part of the project, though, was a Beowulf literary newspaper, which students planned, wrote, and edited in small groups. Newspaper sections included front page, sports, travel, advice column, obituary, comics, and food. Each section was used to summarize and comment on aspects of the Beowulf story. For example, in the sport section of one newspaper we analyzed, the main battle between Beowulf and his enemy, Grendel, was repackaged as a boxing match. The travel section described a fall festival that humorously captured the lifestyle of medieval Scandinavia. The crossword puzzle provided a playful way for students to select and define challenging vocabulary from the story.

Work on the newspaper actually required two readings. On the one hand, students had to read and reread *Beowulf* to make sure they sufficiently understood the plot and details. Then they had to consult modern newspapers, available online, to better understand their genre, content, and formatting. They then had to translate between the two, interpreting the plot, setting, and characters from Beowulf in a newspaper format. Old English stories are not typically of great interest to California junior high students. However, by helping students access background information online and giving them the opportunity to design their own creative modern newspaper on the Beowulf theme, the teacher provided a highly engaging way for these immigrant students to enter into the world of medieval English literature.

Interestingly, the Beowulf story was taught in several of the laptop schools we visited, and in each case teachers made ample use of technology to help students better engage the text. At Flower School in the same district, junior high students went online to read and hear the original Old English version of the poem, thus helping develop their understanding of how language changes over time. Following their reading of the poem, they then composed interpretational music for it using Apple's GarageBand software. At Carlton High, students created an advertising campaign about staying for a night or a weekend in an imaginary hotel where the story takes place, and then presented the campaign to their classmates using PowerPoint. In all of these examples, the classes made use of technology to interpret medieval literature through a modern genre—whether in song, newsprint, or advertisement. The teachers thus leveraged students' interest in modern culture and media as a way to foster engagement with challenging literature. This represented not only an emotive and behavioral engagement, based on students' personal enjoyment at working with new technology, but also a cognitive engagement, as students were required to think about aspects of the literature and how best to convey their medium in an alternate medium.

The Beowulf projects described above all took place in regular language arts classes. Ms. Patterson, in addition to teaching regular English language arts, also taught special sections of language arts for ESL students, and she used similar approaches in those classes. For example, her intermediate ESL class read *Lupita Mañana* (Beatty, 2000), a children's novel about a teenage girl from Mexico who crosses into the United States in order to support her family. Though the topic was of great relevance to their lives, reading an English-language novel still posted a big challenge for these ESL students. To help students interpret the novel, Patterson had the class break into teams to plan and design a movie trailer to advertise an imaginary film based on the book. How the movie trailers were produced will be discussed at more length in Chapter 6, because the creation of the trailer, as well as that of some other products mentioned above (e.g., comic strips and musical compositions), represents a fascinating example of media design in the laptop classroom. For now, though, it is sufficient to emphasize that the instructor's handout, rubric, and organization of class time all were directed at helping the students think about the novel's story line, setting, plot, and characters and how they could be best communicated to an outside audience.

Carlton High: Ms. Gonzales's Ninth-Grade Classes

Carlton High is in a culturally and linguistically diverse middle-class Southern California neighborhood. Most students at the school are academically successful, as evidenced by the school's high test scores, which are in the top decile statewide. Nevertheless, as with other high school adolescents, the students at Carlton still must transition from school-based literacy to the more challenging academic literacies required to succeed in college. The curriculum in Carlton's laptop program is designed to help that transformation.

The laptop program at Carlton is voluntary, with parents having the option of placing their students in the program (almost all students in the program are provided laptops by their parents, but school loaners are available in limited numbers for students who wish to participate but could not otherwise afford to). Students in the program are then assigned to laptop classes (e.g., World History—Laptop), which follow the same curriculum as nonlaptop classes but which take place in wireless one-to-one environments. Interestingly, neither the program at Carlton nor a similar program at nearby Melville High were targeted at the most academically successful students. Those high-achieving students for the most part take Advanced Placement or International Baccalaureate classes, for which no laptop classes are offered. Nor do laptop classes attract the lowest performing students, either because laptop sections are not offered for remedial coursework or because they lack the financial or other support mechanisms at home to join a laptop program. For the most part, average-performing or slightly under-achieving students are enrolled in these voluntary laptop programs, as parents hope to leverage children's interest in technology to improve their school performance.

At Carlton, we observed and interviewed several English teachers, including Ms. Gonzales. The ninth-grade teacher is a technology enthusiast, who had integrated computers into writing courses she taught at a local college for years. New to high school teaching, she took the job at Carlton largely because of the laptop program.

Gonzales integrates laptops into language arts instruction in some ways that are similar to those in the other classes described above. For example, students visit websites to gather background, including a highly irreverent site put out in connection with a film release that features a tabloid-style newspaper about Shakespeare's life and times (Twentieth Century Fox, 1996). She also has students create their own multimedia to analyze language and interpret texts. We witnessed students in her class making PowerPoint presentations of advertisements they had developed for a teen market product that purposely included examples of literary devices and figurative language (i.e., onomatopoeia, alliteration, personification, metaphor, and simile) that students had to master, both as part of the grade-level language arts standards and also in preparation for their work in reading Shakespeare. The other students watched the presentations and pointed out the examples they saw.

Gonzales's class also featured some other creative uses not witnessed elsewhere. For example, with the Blackboard (2005) course management software system used by the school, she was able to create online surveys for students. Before reading *Romeo and Juliet*, the students used a poll to express their agreement or disagreement with statements such as "Parents know what is best for children," "14-year-olds are too young to know when they are in love," and "We always support our friends no matter what." The answers were immediately tabulated with graphs and shown to the class to spark discussion. At the same time, students were asked to write one or two sentences on each poll question, and those answers could be shown on the projector so that all other students could review and respond to them.

Gonzales's was also one of the classes we witnessed that used online discussion forums. Computer-assisted classroom discussion has long been used in college composition classes to spark collaborative interpretation of readings and construction of knowledge (see Warschauer, 1997, 1999). In K–12 classrooms, it is most frequently used in coordination with university-sponsored research projects focused on promoting higher forms of learning (e.g., see Scardamalia, 2003). Teachers at Carlton had access to an online discussion tool through the school's course management software, and the tool was frequently used by Gonzales as well as by other language arts and social studies teachers. Gonzales uses such online discussion either to discuss texts already read or, more frequently, to prepare for readings. For example, before students read O'Flaherty's short story "The Sniper," she asked her students to write and share an online journal imagining what it would be like to live in a place where war was conducted in the streets. A student from the Middle East enriched the discussion by writing about his experiences with conflict in his country. Gonzales believes such online discussion frequently helps draw more reticent students into the analytic process, and indeed, this is consistent with prior research (e.g., see Warschauer, 1997, 1999). Gonzales explained the difference in discussion participation levels:

> In an oral discussion, students one, two, and three always want to share because these are my extroverts. I've got five, six, seven, eight, through twenty who aren't really as confident in speaking. Maybe student twenty is my special kid who has a slur and a more high-pitched voice. He doesn't feel comfortable sharing. Student thirteen back here in the corner is just shy, doesn't like to speak out loud. In a lot of discussions. . .it's not required that every student is interacting or responding. I can have students sit in the back thinking about what he did on the weekend with his paintball game. But in this manner [online discussion], it really is requiring their interaction. I can verify that they've done it.

Gonzales also made use of LessonBuilder, an educational software program leased by the school, to create interactive versions of some readings. For example, she created a 10-page interactive website for "The Sniper" that included a variety of items: background information (e.g., a brief overview of Dublin in the 1920s, a historical timeline, a list of key vocabulary and idiomatic expressions); illustrative maps, diagrams, and photos (e.g., a drawing of the rooftops involved, an early twentieth-century poster listing reasons why you should join the Irish Citizen Army); links to additional explanatory material (e.g., existing websites on the Irish Republican Army, the Easter Rising rebellion of 1916, and the Bloody Sunday massacre of 1972); a classwork assignment (e.g., list the various types of conflict in the story, provide detailed notes on the main characters); and the instructions and rubric for a follow-up assignment (a first-person letter from the sniper to his own son 20 years after the incident described in the story); as well as the text of the reading itself.

In addition to the maps, diagrams, photos, and links described above, two other forms of scaffolding were included within the text of the story. First, brief teacher comments, such as "REFLECT: Characterization" or "WORD USE: Strong verbs," had been interspersed throughout the story for the purpose of drawing students' attention to literacy devices or language that the instructor deemed relevant. Second, pop-up text annotations were hotlinked to words or phrases within the text so that students could get more information by rolling over the link. In some cases the annotations defined difficult words or phrases; in other cases, they offered additional commentary on literary devices, character development, or plot elements.

We were not able to observe these interactive reading lessons during our week of observations at Carlton as other language arts activities were occurring at that time. Gonzales told us that the software was newly leased at the school, and she herself had just begun to develop and make use of such interactive material. It was thus impossible to judge which aspects of the particular lessons we examined, such as the Gonzales's website for "The Sniper," were most or least helpful to students. It seems that, in some ways, it is possible to go overboard in such scaffolding—for example, by providing definitions to students for words that they should be encouraged to guess from context.

But while it is difficult to evaluate the specifics—and indeed, our sense is that Gonzales and the other teachers at the school are themselves in the process of making such judgments—the overall potential of such interactive tools is clear, particularly in regard to students who may not be able to read grade-level material, such as English-language learners. If properly developed, such scaffolded materials should be able to provide just enough support to assist people in reading without proving too distractive. Indeed, through the use of optional pop-ups or multiple versions, teachers and students will be able to select different levels of scaffolding.

It is also important to recognize that the nature of reading is changing. Though the shift of writing from page to screen has progressed further (see discussion in next chapter), the shift of reading to the new medium is also well underway, especially among young people. It's impossible to predict how fast this shift will progress and how far it will reach, but there seems little doubt that the next generation of youth and young adults will be reading more online than the current generation, and probably reading a corresponding less amount of print. This likely means that an increasing proportion of their reading material will be accompanied by images, hyperlinks, and online reference tools. Do such materials make reading easier, especially for young people who are comfortable with computers and screens? Undoubtedly—and the teachers at Carlton report that, when given the choice of receiving printed material or reading the marked-up online materials, almost all the school's students prefer the latter. Is there a mismatch between doing scaffolded reading at school, and then taking tests without such scaffolds? Yes—just as there's a mismatch between using calculators for mathematics or word processing for writing, and then taking a test without those elements (see further discussion in the following chapter on writing). In the long run, though, as the nature of reading, writing, and mathematics change in society, they will similarly change in schools and, eventually, on school exams.

It is also the case that the kind of materials development that Gonzales engages in can be quite time-consuming; not every teacher will be creating lessons as elaborate as she has. But locating, cutting and pasting, and photocopying traditional print materials also takes considerable time, and the end products cannot be so easily shared with other teachers near and far, or so readily revised and edited for new classes or contexts in the future. Most teachers told us that it was actually much more efficient to find and share reading materials online than in print. Though Gonzales put a considerable amount of time into developing her Sniper lesson, the other teachers in the laptop program at Carlton also made use of LessonBuilder to prepare similar materials for their students.

No other schools in our study had access to this kind of interactive materials development software, so we are unable to comment on its use elsewhere. However, teachers at other schools did develop instructional websites for their students, with links to supplementary reading, reference materials, images, and other content to support their reading. We expect that interactive software such as LessonBuilder will become increasingly common in schools—and more diversified. For example, at least one much more elaborate program designed to provide multiple types of text scaffolding for English-language learners is currently under development: e-Lective Language Learning (see Cummins, 1998).

Similarly, no other school had access to the kind of discussion forum software available in Blackboard, though a teacher at Plum High in Maine experimented with a collaborative writing software program (discussed in Chapter 4) and a teacher at Flower School made creative use of a program allowing students to exchange clipboard contents: ClipboardSharing (see Lagercrantz, 2003). With the growing diffusion of course management systems such as Blackboard, free open-source alternatives such as Moodle (2005), and specially designed multiuser knowledge-building software (for examples, see Dede, Clarke, Ketelhut, Nelson, & Bowman, 2005; Scardamalia, 2003), it is reasonable to expect that over time more sophisticated communications and discussion software will make its way into technology-intensive schools.

USING TECHNOLOGY TO PROMOTE READING

Many of the practices at the three schools discussed above were broadly noted across the other laptop classrooms in our study. Some practices were unique to individual schools, but they were still consistent in purpose with the general thrust of how technology was used to promote reading in the one-to-one classroom. We witnessed a few other types of uses in other laptop classes (with some key ones mentioned below), but these uses were also consistent with the general patterns noted in the focal classes. These overall patterns of teaching and learning reading can be summarized in three groups: scaffolding, epistemic engagement, and page-to-screen shift.

Scaffolding

Reading is far more than bottom-up decoding of text from a page. Rather, it is a "psycholinguistic guessing game" (Goodman, 1967) in which readers combine bottom-up information from the text with top-down processing of their broader content and linguistic knowledge, as well as familiarity with the specific texts and genres at hand. It is for this reason that provision of sufficient scaffolding is considered so crucial in reading instruction. Such provision allows students to develop and rely on their broader content and linguistic knowledge, as well as other forms of support (e.g., images), so that they can decipher and understand age-appropriate texts that might otherwise be too difficult for them. This is especially important for the large numbers of students who are not yet able to read English-language materials at grade level, including most students in ESL and special education programs.

One of the main uses of laptops observed in the reading classroom was to help provide such scaffolding. This took place in a variety of ways. First, textual and multimedia material from the Internet was used to help provide general background knowledge on topics related to the reading. This occurred in all the language arts classrooms we visited. Second, technology was used to help promote students' linguistic knowledge. In most classes, students used word processing or presentation software to record, work with, or illustrate vocabulary or literary terms. In some classes, students also engaged in interactive lessons on particular language or grammar points that made use of animated instructional movies (see BrainPOP, 2005). Third, in a few schools, more specific forms of textual scaffolding and support were built into online texts. Teachers at Carlton High used LessonBuilder at Carlton to provide pop-up annotations with supportive information on individual words and phrases. In two schools in Maine, students used text-to-speech software to listen to words they were having difficulty decoding. At several schools, students used online dictionaries or other reference materials. One teacher at Flower School reported that simply taking reading tests and putting them onto the computer increased readability by allowing students to change the font to a larger size. Fourth, the kinds of text analysis that students engaged in at River School and elsewhere—using graphic organizers and other software to map out the elements and characteristics of texts—can be considered another form of scaffolding, by providing students with better tools for understanding how texts are formed and how they convey meaning.

Epistemic Engagement

Student engagement is one of the critical factors leading to success in reading. International test score data indicates that, over time, students whose family background is characterized by low income and low education but who are highly engaged readers will substantially outscore more privileged students who are less engaged readers (Guthrie, 2004). Engaged readers spend more time reading, demonstrate greater enthusiasm and enjoyment of literacy, cognitively process reading material more deeply, and more actively pursue literacy activities inside and outside of school (Cummins, 2005; Guthrie, 2004).

We witnessed a great deal of such engagement with laptops, and these observations of student engagement were confirmed by survey and interview data. Student engagement is also confirmed by most prior research done in laptop classrooms (e.g., see Bebell, 2005; Silvernail & Lane, 2004; Walker et al., 2000). Much of this comes simply from the fact that students enjoy working with computers. It also stems from the broad array of reading materials available online, which can be used to better match student interests, as seen in the comments by the reading teacher specialist at the beginning of this chapter. In fact, the students in that example—and in many other examples we witnessed—became more engaged in reading not only because they were reading online, but also because the technology-enhanced activity they were carrying out interested them so much that they went to whatever source necessary—including print materials—for further reading to complete the task.

The key to this type of engagement is not merely the difference between page and screen (though that too is an important distinction, as discussed below), but also the difference in type of literacy activity, between what Wells and Chang-Wells (1992) refer to as *performative* and *epistemic* literacy activities. In performative literacy activities, texts are used in classrooms so that students can demonstrate what they do or do not know, for example, by reading aloud or providing answers to discrete item questions. In epistemic, or knowledge-building, literacy activities, students work together to interpret and create meaning from texts. In the simple example given at the beginning of this chapter, the two students were examining and illustrating how diagrams, captions, and pictures work through accessing and analyzing written and diagrammed material on a topic of interest to them. In many other examples we observed, students worked to explore and analyze the genres of texts, write for public audiences about texts they had read, and communicate the meaning of texts through alternate modes. As a teacher at Henry Elementary in California told me after her students digitally composed music to a poem they had read, "They had to be very thoughtful and think rhetorically. It wasn't a matter of this was the answer to the question, but what was the emotion going on in the poem. They thought more deeply about the poem."

Of course it doesn't require laptops to carry out such epistemic literacy activities in the classroom. Nor does the presence of laptops guarantee that such activities will take place. Teachers' predilection to such activities is largely a matter of their broader belief, experiences, and skills. For example, each of the three teachers showcased above had a great deal of pedagogical content expertise in the teaching of English language arts, and we expect they would have tried to promote epistemic literacy whether or not they had laptops. However, it is also the case that the wireless one-to-one classroom lends itself to such activities due to the access it provides to online content and to diverse writing, analysis, and media-production software. It is thus not surprising that in our survey of teachers (conducted in three of the schools), 90% agreed with the statement, "Students explore topics in more depth" in the laptop classroom.

Page-to-Screen Shift

The third and final change in instructional patterns in reading that we noted in the laptop classrooms was what we call "page to screen." Simply put, students conducted a higher proportion of their reading activity in computerized environments than ordinarily occurs in the traditional classroom.

Such a finding is obvious, and we would be completely surprised if it were not the case. Nevertheless, there are some elements of this matter worthy of discussion. First, we believe that students gained valuable online reading skills in the process. For the most part, online reading skills were not taught explicitly but were instead embedded into the numerous assignments, many of which required skimming and scanning online content to find specific information or to summarize the main idea. This took place both in language arts classes and across the curriculum, as students in almost every subject area were expected to read material online. (More specific forms of strategy instruction for finding online content will be discussed in Chapter 5.) Of course most youth are frequently accessing the Internet outside of school as well, and they need little encouragement to do so. However, in these classes they were being "socialized" to view the Internet not only as a source of games and chatting, but also as a source of reading material, and were gaining practice in reading online for a variety of specific purposes.

A second point worth mentioning is that only some of the skills they were gaining from these online activities were transferable to offline realms, and particularly to answering the kinds of questions that appear on standardized reading tests. Knowing how to interpret the relationship between textual and audiovisual media, navigate hypertextual material, and effectively use online reference tools are all valuable reading skills for the twenty-first century, but they are not likely to show up on current versions of standardized tests.

The teachers in this study who used laptops best were also highly focused on extensive reading from books. For example, both Ms. Gonzales and Ms. Patterson were among the leaders in their schools in implementing extensive book-reading programs. Nevertheless, it is undoubtedly the case that an increasing focus on the screen inevitably takes time away from the page. This has already happened in business environments, is steadily happening in home environments, and will increasingly occur in school environments. And at least one study (not conducted in laptop classrooms) has found a negative correlation between the amount of time spent using computers for multimedia production in school and English language arts test scores; a similar negative correlation was found between using computers for recreation at home and English language arts test scores (O'Dwyer, Russell, Bebell, & Tucker-Seely, 2005).

For these reasons and others (including the technology learning curve, with most laptop programs still in their infancy), one-to-one laptop programs would not be anticipated to raise reading test scores, especially in the early years of implementation. And that has been confirmed by analysis of data. Reading scores in Maine have remained flat in the 3 years since the laptop program was first implemented (Silvernail, 2005). English language arts scores have on the average risen slightly in the California schools we have researched, but on the whole to no greater extent than for students outside of laptop programs (for further details, see Warschauer & Grimes, 2005).

While laptop programs have not yet raised reading scores, neither have they led to declining scores. Rather, it seems that students continue performing in reading tests at about the same rate as before, while at the same time gaining a broader set of skills, knowledge, and attitudes that in the long run will benefit other aspects of their learning and literacy development beyond those measured by standardized reading tests.

Whether this will change over time as students, teachers, and schools become more accustomed to use of laptops cannot be predicted. In any case, laptops will likely be adopted not because they are proven to raise test scores but because they come to be seen as a vital literacy tool, just as schools adopted other technologies of literacy, whether blackboards or libraries, without awaiting proof via improved test scores.

CONCLUSION

Laptop programs are seldom established with the principal goal of improving reading. At the same time, as one-to-one laptop programs are implemented in schools for a broader range of literacy and learning purposes—including to promote better writing, research, and design skills—such programs also have great potential for reading instruction.

In particular, laptops in the 10 schools we investigated were widely used to provide better scaffolding for readers through access to background and supplementary information and tools for language study. They were also used for epistemic or knowledge-building purposes, as students took advantage of computer software to collaboratively analyze and discuss texts, interpret texts through multimedia, and write and publish about texts they had read.

CHAPTER 4

Writing

> I've been able to do so much more writing, because the whole process is facilitated by the laptops. They do some sort of prewriting on the computer using a graphic organizer. And then they word process and peer edit the rough drafts. And then they word process their final draft. I read the word-processed version, which is really nice, because handwritten drafts are sometimes so hard to read. I do a final editing and say, "Here are a few corrections you need to make." Again, getting that final product—it's so much better, the quality of it. When it was all handwritten, nobody wanted to rewrite the whole paper. That was laborious and tedious. Now, they are accountable for having an even better final product.
>
> —Language arts teacher, Flower School

Even though writing is considered one of the "3 Rs," it has been substantially neglected in U.S. schools (National Commission on Writing in America's Schools and Colleges, 2003). Several factors are now changing that. First, as the United States has transitioned to an information economy, writing today is a requirement for a vast array of occupations, as well as for everyday life. Second, with larger numbers of Americans pursuing higher education, improved writing instruction in schools is required to prepare students for college composition. And third, writing instruction is correctly viewed as valuable toward development of broader thinking skills. Reeves (2002), for example, has investigated what he calls "90/90/90 schools"—defined as highly successful schools with large numbers of low-income and minority students—and has found that they universally place a high emphasis on informative writing.

For all of these reasons, essay writing has surfaced in recent years as a component of both the revised SAT exam as well as high school exit exams in many states throughout the country. Essay writing is also increasingly included in state or district high-stakes assessments. Thus districts, schools, and individual teachers are all under pressure to better prepare their students to write.

Yet writing is extraordinarily hard to teach in a typical K–12 classroom. Effective writing, like reading, involves engagement of background information, and the relatively few informational resources in a classroom limit students' ability to gather background information for their writing. In many cases, students tire easily from writing by hand or suffer from poor handwriting that cannot be easily deciphered by their peers or teachers. It is thus difficult for their teachers to quickly read and reply to their writing. It is even more difficult for students to revise their handwritten papers, as they need to either erase parts by hand or rewrite their entire paper.

Computers and the Internet potentially change all this by providing a wealth of background information for planning writing, as well as a tool for inputting and revising text. Online dictionaries, thesauruses, spell-checkers, grammar checkers, and bibliographic software provide additional support for the writing process, and papers written on a computer are far more legible and thus easier to evaluate and provide feedback on. They also can be submitted to software engines that provide automated essay feedback and scores. The final products are in a format that is more suitable than a handwritten paper for sharing with others, whether via posting on a class bulletin board or making available to others outside the classroom.

With all these potential benefits, it is not surprising that writing papers is one of the two most common uses of laptops in the classrooms we studied, together with browsing the Internet. In the remainder of this chapter, I analyze in more detail the ways that laptops are used in the writing process by examining the concrete experiences of teachers and students.

The writing instruction that we witnessed in laptop schools incorporated two basic principles that are commonly understood in writing pedagogy: first, good writing takes place through a process of multiple stages; and second, during this process, good writers pay close attention to genre (see discussion of process and genre in Badger & White, 2000). I will start by examining the use of laptops in four stages of the writing process—prewriting, writing drafts, rewriting, and dissemination—and then consider more broadly how students learn to write in the laptop classroom

PREWRITING

Prewriting involves thinking about both the subject context (what one knows about the subject matter) and the personal context (what one intends to say about the subject matter; see discussion in Rohman,

1965). It also involves attending to and thinking about the genre one will write in. Teachers in the laptop classroom made use of technology to assist each of these aspects of prewriting.

Background Research

Students frequently consulted the Internet to get background information related to their writing. In some cases, they looked for facts and data that they could incorporate into an argument, thus bolstering their knowledge of the subject context. In other cases, they found images that were related to the topic of their writing, and then engaged in class discussions about these images, thus reflecting on their personal context. For example, Ms. Gonzales at Carlton High in California had her students do online searches for images they were passionate about, and then they discussed the images in class before writing poems about them. In some cases, Ms. Gonzales's students would engage in such discussions orally; in other cases, they would carry such discussions online, to provide opportunities for written reflective discussion before essay writing. This would allow students to try out phrases, ideas, and ways of explaining things in writing before beginning a formal essay. By requiring students to write a certain length and in complete sentences in these online discussions, Gonzales gave her students additional time on task in academic writing.

Graphic Organizers

By far the most common use of technology in prewriting was through use of graphic organizers. Students made use of a variety of software for this, including Inspiration (Inspiration Software, 2005), Smart Ideas, (Smart Technologies, 2006), My Access (Vantage Learning, 2006), or simply AutoShapes in Microsoft Word. These tools provide a variety of scaffolding for planning writing. For example, the essay planning template in Smart Ideas, used at River Elementary in California, prompts students to fill in shapes indicating the thesis statement, the three main ideas, three pieces of evidence for each idea, and a conclusion. Inspiration software, used at Plum High in Maine and Flower School in California, allows students to automatically convert their diagrams into outlines. The prewriting tools in My Access are much more elaborate. For example, they invite students to respond to a variety of written prompts (such as listing the pros and cons of a persuasive argument) and then convert these into essay text.

From our observations, use of such tools did not inspire creativity among students, but that was not the underlying purpose. Rather, teachers sought to drive home the structure of basic five-paragraph essays. As Mr. Molina of River Elementary explained,

> I've tried to teach argumentative essay before, but it's very hard to teach. Having different colors, arrows, shapes, it really helps them see the structure of that. The whole time we were looking at it, we were looking at a student writing model, and we were comparing it to this—they can see the introduction, the evidence, the conclusion. This is just a basic essay, most of the stuff that they write in fourth grade will apply to it. They love it, and I love it too.

WRITING DRAFTS

Laptops were, not surprisingly, used extensively for the actual drafting of written texts. Almost all written work was done on laptops, with three exceptions. First, a minority of students chose to write first drafts by hand and final drafts on the computer. Second, a few teachers preferred that certain work be done by hand for a personal touch. For example, an elementary school teacher at Flower School had her students write weekly handwritten letters to their parents reporting on their progress for a more personal mode of student-parent communication. Third, some teachers occasionally assigned students to write essays by hand to prepare them for state examinations. These teachers, as other teachers we spoke with, believed that writing by computer encouraged a better writing process (e.g., by facilitating more revising), but they felt obligated to at least occasionally offer their students the opportunity to practice writing by hand so as to more closely duplicate conditions similar to those of high-stakes examinations. From our observations, all these exceptions taken together encompassed well under 10% of student instructional writing. The remaining 90% of student instructional writing was completed by computer.

In our observations, interviews, and surveys, we noted two important sets of advantages of drafting by computer (not including ease of revision): the relative physical ease of writing by computer and the types of writing scaffolding available via computer.

Keyboard vs. Hand

Most children find it easier and more enjoyable to write by computer than by hand and thus write at more length on laptops. As a teacher at Henry Elementary school in California explained,

> They are writing more, it's better quality, it's produced faster. I think the laptops facilitate the writing because there is less fatigue involved than with cursive or print. They have the Internet right there to pull up graphics, they have AppleWorks drawings to illustrate their stories, so I think the laptop is a great facilitator of writing. I'll give my students prompts to write a short story, and usually before the stories were 2–3 pages, but this year, their short stories are 8–10 pages long.

Related to this, a frequent point mentioned in student and teacher interviews—and noted in our own observations—was poor handwriting. Students consistently told us that their weak handwriting skills discouraged them from writing, and teachers often pointed to the difficulty of reading students' handwriting.

The difficulty of writing by hand—and thus the corresponding benefit of laptops—is often magnified for students who have special difficulties with coordination, motor skill, or cognitive function. A special education teacher in Maine explained the advantages of laptops for her students:

> [It's been] absolutely phenomenal. For many of our students with cognitive disabilities, getting the ideas from your brain onto paper is pretty much a torture. But whatever reason, and the reasons are as different as the individual students are, word processing as opposed to handwriting has been an incredible tool in terms of creatively being able to express themselves and then also working on just the mechanics of written language. We see it over and over again. It's been a plus. It levels the playing field sort of with their peers. . . .When you're receiving special education services, it's all about alternatives. You don't fit into that little paper and pencil box.

Of course the advantages of writing by computer were multiplied for students who were good keyboarders. We noted that all students picked up keyboarding to some extent, but there was great variation in this matter, largely due to their home experience with computers, the amount of time they had been using computers at school, and whether they had any prior or concurrent formal school instruction in keyboarding or typing.

Scaffolding Tools

A second major advantage of drafting by computer was the various scaffolding tools available in word processing software and on the Internet. Virtually all students used spelling checkers as part of their writing, and many also used grammar checkers, dictionaries, and thesauruses. Of course few students could use all these tools expertly, as the tools themselves require some underlying linguistic knowledge to use well, but most felt that they benefited from them. Several students discussed the underlying learning mechanisms involved, explaining that once a spelling checker, grammar checker, or thesaurus pointed something out to them, they could not only make the change or correction in the current work but would take note of it for the future.

One particularly interesting scaffolding tool we noted was Noodle-Bib (NoodleTools, Inc., 2006), an online bibliographic software tool used at Plum High in Maine. Students used the software program to help create MLA- or APA-formatted reference lists. However, whether or not students used such a tool, in general we noted much more attention to reference lists in the laptop classes than in other typical classrooms we had visited, likely due to the greater ease in creating a correctly formatted, alphabetized reference list when writing by computer than by hand.

Teachers we spoke to had diverse feelings about the use of such scaffolding tools in the classroom. Most lauded them, believing that they provided assistance to students to correct and improve their papers autonomously. One language arts teacher in California went so far as to allow her students to use the spell-checker on their spelling tests if they wished. She believes that students will have access to spell-checkers in the real world and it is thus more important for them to learn how to use them correctly than to function without them. A couple of teachers we spoke with reminisced about the old days, when "hardworking students" learned spelling, grammar, and reference/citation matters without needing to resort to computer-based tools in contrast to the "lazy students" today who overly relied on such crutches. As one teacher explained,

> The better writers came 10, 20 years ago when they really did
> have to use their imagination and really they had to know the

skill. . . .They didn't have to rely on finding it, you know, just
pressing a button and it fixes it for them. They had to know
where to put commas, [how] to place prepositions and to do
those things. Now, most of what they do is at their fingertips. I
see that as a hazard more than a help.

The debate thus mirrors contentions related to computer-scaffolded reading (see Chapter 3) as well as use of calculators in mathematics classes.

REWRITING

It is in the area of rewriting—revising a paper based on feedback from
others or on one's own analysis and thinking—that the power of computers is most evident. It is thus not surprising that the strong majority of both teachers and students we surveyed indicated that students
revised and edited their work more in the laptop classes than they did
in traditional classrooms.

Writing on laptops helped the revising process in three ways. First, it
made the written product more readable and thus easier to evaluate. Second, it provided alternate mechanisms for provision of feedback. Third,
it greatly facilitated students' ease at making changes to papers.

Reading and Evaluating

Word-processed text, whether viewed on the screen or printed out,
was in general much easier to read than handwritten text. This allowed
students better opportunity to review and check their own work. In
several of the schools we observed, teachers encouraged this process
through the use of color coding. We witnessed color coding both on
the screen (using the highlight or font color feature in word processors)
and by hand (using multicolored pens to mark up text that had been
printed out). The latter, of course, could also be accomplished without computers, but the greater readability of word-processed material
made this easier in the laptop classroom. Students worked to highlight
particular elements of sentence or paragraph structure that the course
was focusing on. For example, a high school class in Maine highlighted
all linking verbs and prepositions in their papers and then considered
how they might be limited in number to tighten up their writing. A
junior high class in California color-coded a number of elements that
the teacher stressed needed to be included in their essay, such as thesis
statement, transitional words, examples of "showing, not telling," and
a call to action at the end.

Word processing texts on laptops also allowed other students and teachers greater ease and efficiency at reading and evaluating a text. This often took place at the screen, as pairs of students would work together and comment on each other's work. Or a teacher would comment on student's writing on the screen. It also took place as teachers read and reviewed drafts that were printed out and submitted. As a middle school teacher in California commented, "They're easier to read. Things are clearer and they stand out for me. I can find things a lot easier on the essays when I'm looking for them too." A high school teacher in Maine pointed out that she had read about 100 printed student essays the evening before in an hour and fifteen minutes, but that the same stack would have likely taken her half a day to go through if the papers had been written by hand.

Providing Feedback

The laptop classroom also provided opportunities for the teacher and students to provide feedback on others' writing in addition to immediate feedback during evaluation as described above. In some cases, this was done electronically, as comments were made directly on a document, for example, the Track Changes or Insert Comments features of Microsoft Word. In other cases, this was done by hand, but facilitated by the fact that word-processed essays could be set with wide margins or double line spacing to allow more room for written comments. The most radically different form of feedback we witnessed was through automated writing evaluation, which will be discussed later in this chapter.

Editing and Revising

Most important, once students decided to make changes on an essay, they could do so much more easily by computer than by handwriting. As a middle school student in Maine explained, "If you make a mistake in [hand]writing then you have to write arrows and scribble stuff out, but on the computer you can just delete them and cut things out and paste things where you want." A high school student in Maine agreed:

> If you have an idea on paper you have to scratch it out or write it all over. On the laptop you just delete it. You can copy it and put it somewhere else, then write something else. And if you don't like that, just delete that, put that other thing in. You can make it better.

In the laptop classes we observed, we witnessed a much more iterative and natural writing process than in the typical classroom. Students
frequently and constantly revised their work as they wrote it, deleting
words or sentences, moving text around, and correcting mechanical
errors. They also frequently wrote multiple drafts of their papers. A
typical pattern might involve writing one draft that was then reviewed
by peers, another draft that was reviewed by the teacher, and then a
final draft.

A middle school teacher in Maine summarized some of the differences in the feedback and revision process between the typical and
laptop classrooms:

> As a teacher, the most exhausting part of my job was 1 to 1
> writing conferences, especially when you have the red pen
> out, you can't read their writing, you've got to squeeze in com-
> ments in the lines—two or three of those a day were all I could
> handle. And it was harder for them afterward to go back and
> remember. So when you have the laptop, it's live, it's right
> there, you are editing, you are conferencing together. When I
> need to give them feedback on revisions they needed to make,
> it was easier for them to just take what I offered and go back
> right there and do it.

In our surveys, 78% of teachers agreed that "students revise their
work more on laptops" and 74% of students agreed that "I am more
likely to revise/edit my work when I do it on the laptop." These numbers suggest that increased revision was widespread, but not universal.
Our observations and interviews suggested that broader curricular and
testing structures sometimes impeded extensive revision using laptops. For example, a junior high school teacher in California explained
to us that she simply had too much material to cover to meet state
standards and prepare for high-stakes testing to allow students time
to write multiple drafts of papers. Other teachers indicated that they
sometimes preferred to have students write only one draft to better
mimic conditions of state writing exams.

DISSEMINATION

The final stage of writing is dissemination or publishing. We witnessed
public sharing of student writing in laptop classes in more diverse and
varied ways than in the typical classroom.

Most of the laptop classrooms were "print rich," with student work posted throughout the classroom. In some classrooms, multiple versions of student work were posted—including brainstorming maps, first drafts, and final drafts—to signal the importance of the overall writing process.

On other occasions student work was read aloud. One interesting example we found of this was at Castle Middle School in Maine. Ms. Evans, a language arts teacher there, invited her students to deposit printouts of their creative writing, whether poetry or prose, anonymously into a "ThoughtPot" throughout the week. Every Friday the class sat in a circle while Ms. Evans picked out and read student work. Working with laptops allowed students to write higher quality work (e.g., through more revision), to play with formatting (e.g., through mixing different fonts and spacing in their poetry), and to submit their work anonymously (it could have been identified if written by hand). Later, the students and teacher decided to publish the best work from the ThoughtPot in a book of anonymous poetry.

In another interesting example, students at Henry Elementary School in California read their essays out loud while simultaneously showing a slide presentation they had developed of the figurative language they had used in their paper (e.g., hyperbole, onomatopoeia, similes, metaphors), thereby drawing both their own and their peers' attention to a key linguistic focus of the instructional unit.

Students in laptop classrooms also shared their work with distant audiences. For example, students at several of the schools wrote business letters to authentic audiences. Elementary school students in California wrote consumer correspondence letters to a company asking how chocolate is made and received written response. Middle school students in California wrote business letters to universities and companies to get information about their future studies or careers; they incorporated the responses they got into wall posters and presentations.

Writing for authentic audiences was especially prominent at Howard Middle School in Maine. Students there carried out email exchanges with students in Greece (in English) and in France (in French). In one of the most elaborate and rewarding projects, Spanish-language students at the same school authored, formatted, and printed out children's books in Spanish that were then distributed via a humanitarian organization (Safe Passage, 2006) to children living at the Guatemala City garbage dump.

Such authentic assignments provided a motivation and purpose for student writing. In the projects we witnessed, students worked with great excitement and enthusiasm to produce writing for a real audience, and also paid greater attention to the accuracy of their writing. As a teacher involved in the exchange program with Greece explained,

> It made them more aware of "I need to know how to spell this because someone is going to read this," and I don't want them to think, "Oh, look at the American who wrote this and they don't know how to spell that." That kind of thing made a big difference in their writing, because they really want to know "Is this right?" because they realized they have an audience.

Beyond just focusing on correctness, writing for a real audience allowed students to focus on the readers and their perspective and level, rather than just on getting their words on paper. For example, one student first wrote a paragraph that included a discussion of a Camaro; he then edited it to car after thinking more about what the Guatemalan reader might be familiar with. Another student weighed how to depict the concept of spring, taking into account the different climatic conditions in Guatemala. These are simple but excellent examples of students moving from writer-based to reader-based prose, considered a key developmental step in becoming a good writer (Flower, 1984).

AUTOMATED WRITING EVALUATION

The above changes in the writing process were noted across almost all the schools. In addition to that, there was one writing innovation that was implemented in three California schools we observed that deserves special attention. That was the use of automated writing evaluation (AWE) software.

Though such software has been under development for nearly 40 years, it has only become more commonly used in recent years based on improvements in artificial intelligence and more widespread access to computers (for overviews, see Shermis & Burstein, 2003; Warschauer & Ware, in press). Educational Testing Service has been using its e-rater software system to score essays on the Graduate Management Admissions Test since 1999. K–12 and university classrooms have begun using a variety of automated writing evaluation (also called automated essay scoring) services since the early 2000s.

Though automated writing evaluation does not require laptop computers, its spread in K–12 schools has gone hand in hand with the spread of laptops. Since automated writing evaluation requires that work be submitted via computer, it only becomes feasible when students have

ready access to computers, and a number of districts have thus implemented automated writing evaluation in places where students get
such access either through mobile laptop laboratories or one-to-one
laptop programs.

Three major companies produce commercial automated scoring
systems for the U.S. market: Educational Testing Service produces a
program called Criterion, based on its e-rater scoring engine (Burstein,
2003); Vantage Learning produces a program called My Access, based
on its Intellimetric scoring engine (Elliot, 2003); and Pearson Education leases its scoring engine, the Intelligent Essay Assessor (Landauer,
Laham, & Foltz, 2003), to firms that integrate it into a variety of commercial products.

All three engines generate scores through comparisons, either to
the syntactic, semantic, and discourse features of student essays previously scored by hand (e-rater and Intellimetric) or to the semantic
meanings expressed in a corpus of related textual information (Intelligent Essay Assessor). Based on weighted similarities or differences,
they assign a numerical score; for classroom uses, the score is on
either a 4-point or 6-point scale, in accordance with state testing formats.

The programs also provide differing types and amounts of feedback.
ETS's Criterion program provides individualized diagnostic feedback
on style, organization, and development. My Access provides individualized feedback on spelling, grammar, and word usage (similar to that
provided by Microsoft Word, but in more detail) and generic feedback
on organization and development (e.g., every seventh-grade persuasive
essay receiving a score of 2 receives the same general suggestions on
possible ways to improve organization and development). My Access
also provides detailed individual or class scoring reports to teachers and
includes a variety of student writing tools (e.g., model essays, graphic
organizers, thesaurus, dictionary).

My Access was leased by the Farrington School District and used
extensively by the sixth- and seventh-grade students in the laptop program. Our observations of My Access use focused on Nancy Middle
School, in a predominately low-income Latino neighborhood, and
Flower School, in a predominately upper-middle-income White and
Asian neighborhood. Both teachers and students had a generally positive attitude toward My Access. Seven out of nine language arts teachers surveyed said they would recommend the program to other teachers. (The remaining two indicated the question was "Not Applicable,"
suggesting that they did not use the program enough to make a judg-
ment.) A total of 51% of students agreed that My Access helped im-

prove their writing, as compared to 16% who disagreed and 33% who indicated either "don't know" or "neutral."

In observations, we noted that students were highly motivated by the automated scores. They would shout with joy when they got a high score, and they would look for ways to improve their paper when they didn't think their score was sufficiently high. Students tended to concentrate most of their revisions on mechanical aspects, such as spelling, punctuation, and grammar, but this seemed consistent with what takes place in K–12 schools more generally, with teachers lacking time to work substantially with individual students on broader organizational problems with their writing. The more generic feedback offered by My Access on style, organization, and development was largely ignored by students, especially in the beginning of the year. As the school year progressed, some teachers worked to train students to attend to the broader feedback, requiring students to discuss the feedback in groups or to report on one or two specific organizational recommendations that they would follow.

The average number of drafts that students submitted per prompt was fairly low, due in part to student impatience (students might stop trying to improve their score once they reached what they felt was an acceptable level, or once they ran out of easy ideas on how to do so), but due more to the imperatives of the schedule, with teachers moving on to a new topic or assignment before students had time to submit more revisions.

We witnessed some important differences in My Access between the two schools. At the higher income Flower School, where most students had home Internet access as well as greater language and literacy skills and social support, teachers were better able to integrate My Access into homework. Students could thus be introduced to an essay topic in class and then work on it largely at home over a one-to-two-week period, submitting it for scoring as often as they wished. At the lower income Nancy Junior High, where fewer students had Internet access at home and skill levels were lower, teachers tended to focus instruction during school hours, thus limiting the flexibility of the program.

Overall, we found both benefits and drawbacks to the use of automated writing evaluation in the classroom. In many ways, the use of automated evaluation tended to reinforce formulaic writing, as students dropped colloquial language or nontraditional structures to try to get a high score. At the same time, this emphasis on formulaic writing is not so much a function of automated evaluation software, but rather of the broader nature of writing instruction in K–12 schools. Our mass education focuses on teaching the basics of writing, such as how to structure a five-paragraph essay, and technologies are chosen and implemented so as to reinforce that goal.

The use of automated scoring systems could also be seen as contradicting one of the major potential advantages of computer-based writing discussed above—that it allows for more authentic writing activities directed at real audiences. However, all the classes we observed used a combination of writing activities, with some scored on My Access prompts and others for more natural and authentic purposes, thus providing a balance in writing instruction.

A major advantage of automated writing evaluation was that it engaged students in autonomous activity while freeing up teacher time. Teachers still graded essays, but they could be more selective about which essays and which versions they chose to grade. In many cases, teachers allowed students to submit early drafts for automated computer scoring and a final draft for teacher evaluation and feedback. A teacher at Nancy summarized some of the strengths and weaknesses of automated writing evaluation in the classroom:

> I think it makes teaching easier. It's like another pair of eyes, however good or bad those eyes are. It's still much better than what I could do by myself. I have to monitor it, but you have to monitor everything, because I am responsible totally for what goes on in the class. I can't just leave it to something else, and you turn it on, and it puts it into their brain, and then you're done.

Like many of the literacy technologies discussed in this book, we expect the use of automated evaluation software to become more prominent as time goes on. Scoring and feedback engines will be improved, the number of writing prompts will expand, and software will likely become less expensive. In addition, there will likely be a learning curve attached, with students growing accustomed to understanding automated feedback as they similarly grow accustomed to other types of computer scaffolding (such as spelling or grammar checks). Unlike some critics (e.g., Cheville, 2004; Conference on College Composition and Communication, 2004), we don't view automated writing evaluation as an insidious development that will strip away the human element from writing instruction. Good writers already make use of some automated feedback tools, such as spelling and grammar checkers, and the expansion of these tools to include more detailed feedback and numerical scores need not in and of itself raise any alarms. The main point to bear in mind is that such automated systems do not replace good teaching but should instead be used to support it. This is particularly so with the instruction of at-risk learners, who may lack the requisite language and literacy skills to make effective use of automated feedback. Students must learn to write for a variety of audiences, including not only computer scoring engines, but peers, teachers, and interlocutors outside the classroom, and must also learn to accept and respond to feedback from diverse readers.

SUMMARY

As described above, the daily use of laptops in the wireless classroom had a major effect on instruction at each stage of the writing process, including prewriting, drafting, rewriting, and dissemination stages. These changes took place in all the laptop schools we observed, with additional shifts occurring in three schools that deployed automated writing evaluation.

What then was the overall significance of these changes when examining the teaching and learning of writing? We can point to seven overall differences between how writing is, for the most part, taught in laptop classrooms as compared to typical classrooms: Writing became better integrated into instruction; more iterative; more public, visible, and collaborative; more purposeful and authentic; and more diverse in genre. Students' written products improved in quality, and student writing became more autonomous.

Integrated Into Instruction

The advantages of using computers for teaching writing are so compelling that teachers in many K–12 schools try to use them, even if it means rotating students to a few computers in the back of the class, or waiting until a computer laboratory or mobile laptop carts becomes available. However, when all students have their own laptop, computer-based writing can be integrated into instruction much more easily. A language arts teacher at Flower who had previously taught at a school with mobile laptop carts explained the difficulty in using computers for writing there.

> It's huge. If you look at your week, and my day was Wednesday [for mobile laptop cart use], in that setting you throw every-

thing out because I've got my iBooks here today. If you don't start and finish something, it's going to be another week before you get the iBooks. And you don't know what happens to those computers during the rest of the week. There were cases where kids dumped files. Maybe you had a student that didn't finish something. The next week they get that computer, and their stuff is gone. There were lots of mishaps when you only have the computer once a week. Here, it's so much easier to use. They can write 15 minutes a day if you want, and continue writing at home. They can work on it a little bit any time and finish it later.

This kind of integrated writing extended beyond the language arts classroom period into other subjects as well. For example, in the middle school technology course at Flower—a course that all students took to improve their computer and digital media skills—almost every assignment also incorporated some writing. Students designed newspapers and wrote short articles for them, wrote a synopsis of *Echo and Narcissus* for book covers they designed for the story (which they had read in language arts class), and wrote a variety of poems set to digital images. Similar integration of writing in the curriculum took place in the social studies, science, and health courses at Flower and other schools.

Iterative Process

A second change that took place was that writing became much more iterative, with students better able to plan their writing, gather diverse information and resources for it, review and revise their writing, and disseminate or publish it. Helping students understand and develop a good writing process is a goal of both K–12 and higher education, but one that is difficult to achieve without sufficient access to technology. In the laptop classes, working on writing as an ongoing iterative process came naturally.

Public, Visible, and Collaborative

A third change was that writing became more public, visible, and collaborative. Whether on students' individual laptop screens, shown to the class via a video projector, printed out, or shared via electronic communication inside or outside the classroom, writing done on a computer was much more visible and easily shared than that done by hand. For example, Natalie, a student at Carlton High in California, provided an interesting illustration of this point. She explained how she and her classmate sometimes help each other:

> My friend who sits with me at my table, Felicia, we'll go back and forth. If I'm not sure how to start my essay out, I'll start reading hers, and I'm like, "OK, now I see what the teacher wants" and then I'll just take it from there. I don't copy what she writes, but it gives me an idea how I should write my paper.

Natalie further explained that such collaboration wouldn't happen in a typical classroom: "Not a lot of people have very legible writing. . . .The intention [to share] might be there, but when you get the piece of paper, you just can't read it."

Our observations in both the laptop classes and typical classes confirmed Natalie's perspective. We much more frequently saw two or more students gathered around a screen examining or collaborating on student writing in a laptop class than we saw in typical classrooms. For example, another teacher at Carlton assigned students to work in pairs to write a prequel to a story they had read. The greater visibility of the screen allowed one student to keyboard while both could clearly see what was being written and suggest further edits or additions.

And other types of sharing that took place—such as via a video projector or an online discussion forum—are simply not possible in a typical classroom. We witnessed a fascinating example of collaborative online writing in an English class at Plum High in Maine. Students who had read short stories worked in small groups, each sitting at his or her own laptop, to collaboratively author an alternate version of the story from a particular character's perspective. Students used the shareware program SubEthaEdit (Coding Monkeys, 2005) that allows multiple Macintosh users to edit the same document in real time, with each user's contribution appearing in a different color. Though what students learn from such an experience may or may not help them on a standardized writing test, such forms of multivocal writing are becoming increasingly common in the real world and learning how to accomplish such collaboration well is a valuable skill.

Purposeful and Authentic

A fourth change was that writing became more purposeful and authentic. There were certainly exceptions to this, such as the papers written for automated essay scoring as discussed above. But in general, laptop classrooms—including the same classes that sometimes used automated essay evaluation—included multiple opportunities to write for real audiences, whether for poetry readings, long-distance exchanges with students in other countries, publishing of creative writing or children's books, letters to companies and universities, or, as discussed in Chapter 3, online book reviews.

One small but interesting example of this takes place at Castle Middle School in Maine. Students at Castle have the opportunity to participate in video production teams (see discussion in Chapter 6), but in order to do so they have to submit a written application, including a cover letter and a résumé. Students in school are often asked to write letters and, occasionally résumés, but here is an example where how skillfully they do so will have an important impact on whether the student will be able to fulfill a desired task. The goal is not so much to weed out the bad writers—students are given support in writing their letters and résumés and additional criteria are also used to ensure broad participation—but rather to give students an authentic purpose for their writing.

Diverse Genres

Students also had the opportunity to write in a greater diversity of genres and formats in the laptop classroom. As elsewhere, we witnessed all the required genres of essay writing (narrative, expository, persuasive, descriptive). We also witnessed a great variety of other written genres and formats. At Freedom Middle School in California, students read about Thomas Paine's *Common Sense* and then wrote their own pamphlet about conditions in their school. At Carlton High, students used an interactive website to learn about and create haiku poetry. At Nancy Middle School, students wrote an information brochure about their school for distribution to incoming students. At Flower School, students wrote detailed laboratory reports as a requirement of their science experiments. Students at multiple schools designed and wrote newspapers, business letters, magazine advertisements, or journal entries.

Most of this diverse writing would have been very difficult to achieve without computers. Using laptops and the Internet, though, students were able to examine and critique prior exemplars (e.g., perusing other business plans or informational brochures), gather the information they needed to produce their own piece, and format their product appropriately. They could also post it online or share it with others when appropriate, for example, by emailing copies of business letters to companies.

Quality Products

Students produce higher quality written documents in the laptop classroom. This applies to both traditional essays as well as some of the other forms of writing mentioned above. Three main factors appear to contribute to this higher quality: support tools, feedback and revision, and formatting.

1. *Support tools* include spelling checkers, grammar checkers, thesauruses, dictionaries, graphic organizers, bibliographic tools, and search engines. These tools allow students to gather more information for their writing, check their facts, view other exemplars, plan their essays, check or modify their language, and correctly format references and citations.
2. *Feedback and revision* refers to the greater amount of feedback that students get on their writing—due to its increased readability by teachers or peers or the availability of computer-generated feedback—and the greater ease of editing and revision.
3. *Formatting* refers to how students can make their computer-written documents look clean, neat, and professional, in comparison to documents written by hand.

The relative value of formatting is somewhat debatable, of course. On the one hand, formatting has always been an important part of the writing process; consider, for example, how often job seekers have been urged to make sure their résumés look right. If anything, its value has increased in the computer age, when fewer people rely on secretaries to type their work and instead must prepare documents themselves. Even academic manuscripts, which are not meant to be published but just seen by an editorial staff and reviewers, may leave a poor impression or be rejected out of hand if they have inappropriate margins, line spacing, or fonts. Yet on the other hand, students can easily get overly involved in making a document look attractive, without focusing on the underlying content (see discussion in Warschauer, 1999). In the laptop classes we visited, this potential contradiction was well managed; students were given the opportunity to format their papers correctly, but the main emphasis was on the written content. And a number of the teachers went to lengths to make sure students' documents looked professional, rather than flashy. As a science teacher at Nancy Junior High explained,

> I started focusing on [the point that] your margins need to be one inch. This is where your name goes. This is where the

period goes. This is where the title goes, showed them how to center it, how many spaces after the title. You need to indent. All documents cannot be larger than fourteen font, standard is twelve or twelve point. We talked about font because at first I was getting all of these papers that were typed, but they were in this immaculate font and bubble letters and stuff. I had pink and blue. One paragraph was pink. The other one was blue. So now I say, no, none of that. It has to be a standard font and we went over which ones were standard. It has to be in black. It has to be double-spaced. They really get it now. I very rarely get documents that are not how they should be, standard.

Interestingly, the use of automated writing evaluation provided a further counterbalance against a possible overattention to appearance, as the AWE scoring engines all ignore how an essay is formatted.

Autonomous

Finally, students became more autonomous in their writing in the laptop classroom. On the one hand, they learned to use the above-mentioned tools to independently address their writing challenges. As a student at Carlton explained, "A lot of the time [Microsoft] Word will catch a minor grammar mistake that you make, so you learned where you screwed up without the teacher actually having to teach you it." In some schools, students also used feedback from AWE programs without having to wait for a teacher response.

Mostly, though, students just had a highly portable tool that they could use to write and publish their work. For example, in Ms. Evans's class at Castle Middle School we observed students arriving to class early after lunch or recess and opening their laptops before the bell to work on their poetry or prose for the ThoughtPot. We also interviewed students at several schools who engaged in creative writing outside of class, including a student at Plum who regularly posted her work at GreatestJournal.com and two students at Flower who wrote original plays and submitted them to a public contest. A parent at Howard Middle School in Maine explained how her daughter used the laptop outside of school:

She'll use it more now for what I call creative writing. I don't think it's true homework assigned. She does a lot of fictional pieces with dialogue, particularly what I call pure age type writing for fiction, but she'll complete a story that has a really good beginning middle and end. And I haven't seen her print off of it but I think there's a way for it to hook up to our computer at home to print. She enjoys that and she enjoys that it's her responsibility in that it's hers and she watches out for it.

Of course two caveats are in order when considering this autonomy. First, there is no guarantee that some of these independent writing activities were solely due to the laptops. Many youth these days engage in fan fiction and other types of independent writing without school-provided laptops (see Black, 2005). However, our observations and interviews suggested that the provision of laptops provide more students the tools, skills, and disposition to be able to write autonomously.

Second, in spite of this broader access, learner autonomy still depended to some extent on the broader resources that students were able to bring to bear, including language and literacy skills, keyboarding ability, knowledge of computers, and social resources at home. For every student we witnessed who autonomously mastered new skills, there were other students unable to use a spellchecker correctly due to limited reading proficiency. Thus while laptops were a valuable tool for promoting writing, they were certainly not a magic bullet that could overcome all other academic obstacles.

A NEW TYPE OF WRITING

In every school we visited, the teaching and learning of writing represented the content area in which laptops were most consistently and frequently used. Our observations, interviews, surveys, and examination of student work all indicated that writing was also an area in which students most benefited from using laptops. And our findings in this are supported by other studies examining laptop use and writing instruction (e.g., Bebell, 2005; Russell et al., 2004; Silvernail & Lane, 2004). Yet, as with reading, there is no evidence that laptop use significantly correlates with higher test scores on standardized writing tests. Again, the strongest evidence for this is in Maine, where 2 years of a statewide laptop program resulted in only the tiniest gain in eighth graders' writing test scores (with average scaled scores increasing from 537 to 538; see Maine Department of Education, 2005).

I believe the explanation for this contradiction lies in a statement by Peg Syverson, Director of the Computer Writing and Research Lab at the University of Texas, Austin:

Can I prove that online writing courses improve students' ability to write traditional essays? No, I can't. I also can't prove that driver's ed courses improve students' equestrian ability. . . .What we're doing is preparing students for the kinds of writing they need in the future. (quoted in Warschauer, 1999, p. 155)

High-stakes writing tests take place in a single sitting with pencil and paper, in response to decontextualized prompts, and without any additional resources or assistance. Authentic writing in today's world is dramatically different. It is virtually always done by computer, taking advantage of a variety of computer-based tools and, in many cases, drawing on information from the Internet. It is usually done over time, with writers thinking about their message and continually revising their text. It is also often done collaboratively, either through coauthorship or by responding to feedback and suggestions from others. The laptop classes we witnessed without doubt helped better prepare students for these real-world writing tasks. We expect that in some particular contexts (e.g., those schools or districts that use laptops in a very focused effort to improve test scores), there may be some gain in writing test scores as well. But to focus exclusively on test scores to the exclusion of other elements would be to blind ourselves to the true benefits of learning to write with computers.

CHAPTER 5

Information and Research

I always started out before thinking it has to all come from me, I have to be the center. What I tend to do now, though, is give them a background, give them a core of information, or show them where to find the background information, or show them how to evaluate the information I give them, or use the media to evaluate what's happening. I really think in laptop class it is going to be student-centered because you have a laptop and it can take them anywhere. It's more teacher as a facilitator. I'm a tool they can use, too, but there are so many other tools, and they need to know how to utilize all of the tools. So the curriculum is like a vehicle to teach them how to utilize the resources and utilize them to create products that are useful for their learning. And ultimately when they are adults out there, no matter what job they happen to be in or whatever they do with their lives, they need to be able to utilize any resources they're exposed to. It's more of a focus on what students can do with these tools to enhance their learning. And they enjoy that. They like to have control and it really does allow them to be in control.

—Social studies teacher, Melville High School

We are swimming in information. According to one very rough estimate, the maximum amount of information available to any individual has grown from 10^7 bits in the prelanguage era, to 10^9 bits in the era of language, to 10^{11} bits in the era of writing, to 10^{17} bits in the era of print, to 10^{25} bits in the digital era (Robertson, 1998). Information and communication technologies have not only made much more information available, but they have served to obliterate or make irrelevant many of the traditional filters of information. A half century ago, most of the textual information a child came in contact with had been twice filtered: once by editors or publishers, who decided what was worthy of being printed, and once by librarians, parents, or other gatekeepers, who decided what printed material should be made accessible. Children today can gain access to a vast amount of information online that is untouched by either of these traditional filters.

The same digital media that have allowed such a burst of information access have also helped fuel a new stage of industrial capitalism.

This stage, termed *informationalism* by Castells (1996), involves an economic shift from material production to information processing activities—as witnessed by the growth of telecommunications, software, real estate, media, and finance industries—and an increasing role of science, technology, and information management in the production process. It is this economic shift that gives rise to the power of the symbolic analysts discussed in Chapter 1. Productivity and economic success are now largely dependent on the ability to identify and solve problems and create new knowledge through manipulation of information, and those who are most skilled at these activities are highly valued in the labor market.

These two realities—the large amounts of unfiltered information now available and the growing importance of being able to work with information in the production of knowledge—have focused attention on the necessity for *information literacy*. The American Library Association (2000), which has developed competency standards for information literacy, defines it as incorporating six abilities:

- Determine the extent of information needed
- Access the needed information effectively and efficiently
- Evaluate information and its sources critically
- Incorporate selected information into one's knowledge base
- Use information effectively to accomplish a specific purpose
- Understand the economic, legal, and social issues surrounding the use of information, and access and use information ethically and legally (pp. 2–3)

An international panel brought together by Educational Testing Service developed a very similar definition to that of the American Library Association, identifying five critical components of what they termed *ICT Literacy*:

- *Access* — knowing about and knowing how to collect and/ or retrieve information.
- *Manage* — applying an existing organizational or classification scheme.
- *Integrate* — interpreting and representing information. It involves summarizing, comparing and contrasting.
- *Evaluate* — making judgments about the quality, relevance, usefulness, or efficiency of information.
- *Create* — generating information by adapting, applying, designing, inventing, or authoring information. (International ICT Literacy Panel, 2002, p. 3)

These definitions broadly parallel those put forward by other organizations (e.g., American Association of School Librarians & Association for Educational Communications Technology, 1998). There is thus broad agreement on what information literacy entails. At the same time, though, there is disagreement as to the extent to which it is being achieved in schools, and the helpfulness of school technology use for that purpose. On the one hand, there are techno-pessimists, such as Stoll (1995, 1999) and Oppenheimer (1997, 2004), who believe that ready access to computers and the Internet in schools serves to discourage critical thinking by swamping our students in quick and easy information. On the other hand, there are techno-optimists, such as information technology industry representatives, who highlight only the most positive examples of computer use for knowledge production and thus imply an almost automatic correspondence between technology deployment and the development of information literacy (e.g., see Apple Computer, 2006; Intel, 2006; Microsoft, 2006).

Our research at the laptop schools suggests that, not surprisingly, the truth lies somewhere in between. On the one hand, students in the laptop schools universally learned to access information, manage it, and incorporate it into their written and multimedia products. On the other hand, the focus on evaluating information, understanding its social context, and analyzing it for the purpose of knowledge production varied widely across schools.

I will proceed with two broad comparisons. First, I will take the laptop schools as a group and discuss how information literacy practices and research activities in the laptop schools differ from those in typical classrooms. I will then offer some comparisons among laptop schools, to demonstrate how different contexts and approaches combine to yield differing strategies on promoting information literacy and research skills.

INFORMATION AND RESEARCH IN LAPTOP SCHOOLS

Students in laptop schools had access to a much greater variety of information than do typical students. According to our surveys and those of others (e.g., Bebell, 2005; Silvernail & Lane, 2004), gathering information online is one of the most frequent educational activities carried out with laptops. In addition, individual laptops can be a tool for gathering data (e.g., when attached to scientific probes) and for analyzing data (e.g., through spreadsheets and graphing software).

This ongoing access to tools for gathering and analyzing information and data brought about five important changes in instruction: It allowed more just-in-time learning, more individualized learning, a greater ease of conducting research, more empirical investigation, and more opportunities for in-depth learning. Each of these five changes will be briefly discussed.

Just-in-Time Learning

Cognitive scientists have long known that people learn best when information or instruction is provided at the point of need (see discussion in Gee, 2003). Yet this important learning principle is difficult to implement in a typical classroom, when a teacher cannot necessarily anticipate every learning opportunity that may emerge, or, even if anticipated, may not have the opportunity to locate and reproduce materials on the topic.

Just-in-time learning occurred with great frequency in the classrooms we observed. Language arts students went online to find information or images to clarify confusing terms or concepts they came across in medieval literature. Science students consulted revolving 3-D models of DNA to answer questions that came up in class. And social studies students frequently sought out information regarding current events related to classroom discussion.

Teachers often refer to this process as taking advantage of "teachable moments." The phrase was used a number of times in our interviews. Discussing the value of just-in-time learning for her highly curious third graders, a teacher at Flower School in California explained:

> The kids have so many questions and the computer just opens a brand new world. It used to be if a teachable moment arose, then "well, tomorrow we'll find out about that." Now it's "OK, would you open your computer and let's go find out," and we can take them right now and they get excited about it. Right now, we are doing a study on symbols of our nation. We go search the Statue of Liberty. We can take a virtual tour of the White House, or Congress, or the Supreme Court. They can go there and be a part of it. And they could not get out before. They had to rely on the books that were just meant for every student in every state across the nation.

At the opposite end of the K–12 spectrum, several high school teachers discussed the value of students' accessing information on the Internet just when they need it. An English teacher at Melville High in California explained that he never felt so empowered as a teacher until now when he can introduce his students to diverse poets, even those not included in the student's textbook, because his students can access a wealth of poetry on the Internet. A social studies teacher at the same school went to some length in explaining how just-in-time learning has transformed his teaching:

> When I initially started the [laptop] program, I didn't think that it was going to have that much of an effect. I kept thinking, well this will be fun to try, but I still need to use the textbook and I still need to go over all the curriculum and I need to cover these areas. What I found was, literally in my first two years, I almost had to rewrite the curriculum. It was just that I had a door totally open up to me in terms of culture, geography, current events, news, all of the things that I have been trying to get my students to learn from a textbook: language, what this sounds like, what that looks like, these five different cultures that live in one square mile, this civil war, that political situation. All these things that I've been trying to use, pretty much without my hands on, became literally at their fingertips. I would say from the first two years I was teaching Cultural Geography 'till now, they're learning something totally different than my students did in the first two years. We literally have a globe at our fingertips. That's the difference. I can make the Zulu tribe in South Africa come alive for them, versus talk about these people that they've never seen, they don't know, they can't grasp. And where I was using a newspaper of the previous day's news to deal with current events, we can literally track an event hour by hour online and change the discussion minute by minute. It totally involves them one hundred percent in the news.

The views of these teachers were typical of what we found in the laptop classroom. One of the greatest benefits of one-to-one learning, in teachers' eyes, is the wealth of information that can be brought into the classroom at the time students can best make use of it.

Individualized Learning

Another advantage of information access we witnessed in the laptop classroom was more individualized learning. Because of the vast array of content available online, teachers found it much easier to individualize instruction.

One very simple example of this occurred in a social studies class in Maine, where students went online to peruse political cartoons once a week (see Cagle, 2006). The teacher explained that, prior to the laptop program, she picked out one or two cartoons herself to show to the class. But with one-to-one laptops, students were able to search out cartoons they found particularly interesting and then take turns explaining them to the rest of the class.

Another excellent illustration of individualization occurred in a third-grade class in California that included students at a wide variety of reading levels. The teacher created a tic-tac-toe sheet of nine follow-up activities for each reading assignment. Taking advantage of computers and the Internet, students thus had a great deal of flexibility as to which and how many of the nine follow-up activities to complete. This approach allowed students at all levels to complete the activities they were capable of.

One example with interesting cultural implications occurred at Castle School in Maine, where we witnessed a student from Somalia working by herself in the library where she was browsing a website on alcohol and drugs. She explained that the rest of her health class was receiving sex education instruction, but since her mother would not permit her to participate, she was doing individualized substitute research on her own.

Ease of Research

Perhaps the most valuable aspect of information access in the laptop classroom is how it facilitates student research. Teachers and students pointed to several factors about the Internet in facilitating student research. First, the Internet has far more information than most school libraries. Second, the information on the Internet is more current, an important factor given the rapidity of scientific development and social change. As one student told us, "the [print] encyclopedias in our library are from the 1990s, so the newer information is on the Web." Third, it is often much easier and faster to find information on the Internet than in a library. Fourth, the Internet can be accessed directly from the classroom and, for many students, at home as well. Fifth, it is easier to manage, archive, and copy information from the Internet than information in print (though the last point can sometimes be a disadvantage as well as an advantage). And finally, one-to-one Internet access makes teachers' jobs much easier, as they don't need to spend as much time tracking down print resources and photocopying them for the classroom.

For example, Ms. Sharpe, a health teacher at Nancy Junior High in California, assigned her students a research project on school violence. The students gathered information for the study from websites recommended by the teacher with current data, articles, and cartoons on violent acts in schools. Ms. Sharpe told me that, without the laptop program, such a research project would have been very difficult to arrange. As she explained,

> Most of that information [on school violence] is compiled through various agencies and it would have been really hard and really time consuming to do that research in any other way. I don't think there would have been another way other than me researching it and printing it out for them.

Of course the very ease of finding information online creates special challenges for learning how to sort through, select, evaluate, and make use of such a wealth of content. A number of the schools developed special information literacy training modules, sometimes with the assistance of the school library, as illustrated later in this chapter in the discussion of Howard Middle School in Maine. Depending on the students' age and literacy level, teachers also provided appropriate forms of scaffolding. For example, in the school violence research project discussed above, which was carried out among seventh-grade students including many English-language learners, the teacher directed students to 12 preselected websites on school violence, rather than just setting students loose to search the Internet themselves. In other cases, teachers make use of specialized search engines for schools, such as NetTrekker (Thinkronize, 2006), or set up guided information-seeking activities called WebQuests (Dodge, 2005).

Another potential problem with ease of research is plagiarism. Teachers came up with various strategies for discouraging plagiarism. One science teacher in Maine explained that she likes taking two events that seem unrelated and assigning students to write about the commonalities and the differences. She finds that that forces students "to do something that you can't get from anywhere else. It has to come from your head." Along the same vein, other teachers explained that their research assignments require students to give their opinion and support it by citing facts. Since the students spend a lot of preparatory time in class developing and sharing their opinions, the teacher believes this discourages cutting and pasting from the Internet.

In our own somewhat limited observations—we could not read all the essays of the many thousands of students in the schools we visited—we did not witness blatant attempts at plagiarism, that is, trying to pass off someone else's work as one's own. We did, however, sometimes witness students lazily cutting and pasting information from the

Internet into their products (posters, slide presentations, and so on) without citing a source for the material. Unfortunately, such behavior was occasionally abetted by teachers who were so impressed that students had created a nice-looking poster or presentation that they didn't bother to critique the included textual content.

Empirical Investigation

The use of one-to-one laptops also provided greater opportunity for students to work directly with data themselves. By gathering and analyzing data, they could engage in more direct forms of experimentation and research than the second-hand research common at typical K–12 schools.

Sometimes the data they analyzed came from the Internet. For example, at Freedom Middle School in California, a one-to-one laptop program was launched in the alternative education program as a way of trying to better connect to students who were on the verge of dropping out or failing out of school. The teacher there actively sought ways to relate instruction to the students' personal lives. One particularly interesting research activity involved students going to websites that had both test scores and demographic data from schools in the district. Students drew on this data to make charts comparing test score outcomes to income levels (as measured by percent of students receiving free or reduced lunch in particular schools). The activity involved students in animated and thoughtful discussion about what factors might lead to the high correlation between these two measures. It drew students into the intellectual issues involved much more readily than if the teacher had prepared a lecture on the topic of school equity without involving students in actively looking at data related to their own lives and community.

In other cases, students collect the data themselves, for example, by conducting surveys of classmates or taking measurements of objects or events in the classroom and using spreadsheets or online graphing tools (e.g., National Center for Educational Statistics, 2006) to analyze the data. For more sophisticated forms of data gathering, some of the schools purchased scientific probes. For example, the science teacher at Flower School in California had access to a set of digital probes and microscopes that attached to the laptops for gathering and uploading data related to temperature, voltage, light, force, motion, and chemical composition. In one lesson we observed, seventh-grade students worked in groups to measure each other's heart rates in various states (sitting, standing, jumping) and upload the data to computers where it was plotted into graphs. In the process, they developed and tested hypotheses about the effect of various combinations of activity and rest on heart rate.

Finally, online simulation software provided another form of hands-on, interactive learning for students in the one-to-one programs. Students in classes we observed carried out simulated frog dissections (see Froguts, 2006), performed virtual open heart surgery (see Columbus Medical Association Foundation, 2006), and witnessed simulated cell mitosis and meiosis (see Quill Graphics, 2006).

In-Depth Learning

Most of the teachers in our study believed that continuous online access contributed to more in-depth learning in the classroom. In our survey, for example, fully 90% of teachers agreed that "students in laptop classes explore topics in more depth"; 85% of teachers expressed agreement with the statement that "students in laptop classes get more involved in in-depth research."

A common belief in this regard—and one we saw illustrated frequently in the classroom—was that Internet-connected laptops offered students many alternative ways for attacking an issue or problem, thus allowing students to explore a topic more deeply than in a typical classroom. We witnessed a good deal of project-based work, consistent with what many scholars have said best brings out the potential of technology use in the classroom (see discussion in Becker, 2000a; Sandholtz et al., 1997).

A teacher in the Gifted and Talented Education (GATE) program at Henry Elementary School in California, Mr. Spratt, shared his thoughts on the matter, which were consistent with what we observed in the class.

> A great benefit is being able to integrate across the curriculum. In the GATE classes, we work on the issues of depth and complexity—how to notice patterns, trends, details, rules, different perspectives, big ideas. Now, I can integrate better across the curriculum, go deeper. I can also emphasize some of the scholarly attributes we are trying to promote, like showing curiosity, showing academic humility, being prepared with learning tools, considering multiple points of view.

To illustrate this point, Mr. Spratt discussed two interesting math projects his third/fourth-grade class carried out. In one of the projects, discussed at greater length in Chapter 6, students went online to find the California mathematics standards for second grade, worked in groups to design and create games that could help teach these standards, and videotaped themselves providing instruction to the second-grade class on how to play the games. In the second project, students were given fictitious thousand dollar accounts to buy holiday gifts for their friends and family. The students then went online and did comparison shopping from nine different stores, calculated tax according to appropriate parameters, designed their own checks and made simulated purchases, created and updated charts with information about their purchases, made graphs of their spending patterns, designed and produced a poster board on the project incorporating their diverse materials, and wrote reports about the project. In a related activity, they also analyzed the geometric patterns and features of the poster board they had created. Mr. Spratt explained that he had attempted to carry out this holiday math project in previous years but prior to the laptop program "I basically had to hand-feed them a lot of the information." Now armed with laptops, they were able to approach holiday shopping from a wider range of math-related angles and go into the topic in more depth.

VARIATION AMONG SCHOOLS: THE AMPLIFICATION EFFECT

The five pedagogical changes discussed above were general patterns we noticed across the laptop schools. At the same time, there was also a good deal of variation among schools. Some schools were highly successful in promoting information literacy, research skills, and in-depth learning with laptops. Other schools were moderately successful. And in a few cases, we observed teaching and learning that could best be described as shallow.

We believe that these differences can be explained by an *amplification effect* (see discussion in Warschauer, 2000a). Simply put, those teachers and schools that began with strong instructional programs for critical inquiry and research were able to make use of laptops to magnify the success of such instruction. Those schools that began with a weaker focus on inquiry and research had less success in even developing the basics of information literacy. The distinction between strong and weak schools in this regard tended to correlate with socioeconomic status. Schools in high-SES neighborhoods in this study, as in general, tended to have a more experienced teaching and administrative staff, a community of parents with higher educational expectations, and a student population that had been primed since an early age to prepare for college. All these factors tended to contribute to a stronger research focus at the high-SES neighborhood schools than at their low-SES counterparts. At the same time, important exceptions existed, with some of the low-SES neighborhood schools doing an excellent job of promoting information literacy and developing student research skills.

To illustrate the wide variation in approaches to information literacy and research, we briefly look at three laptop schools in Maine: Howard Middle (high SES), Plum High (low SES), and Castle Middle (low SES). Most well-populated states feature dichotomous divides between rundown inner cities with large numbers of minorities (particularly Blacks and Latinos) and well-off suburban areas that are mostly populated by Whites. Maine, however, with a 97% White population, relatively few nonnative speakers of English, and no cities of more than 65,000 people, is not known for this traditional urban-suburban split. Rather, the main social divide in the state is between the relatively prosperous south, which has a number of small cities and coastal resorts and is within commuting distance of Boston, and the struggling north, which is rural, sparsely populated, and has traditionally depended on extraction industries such as logging for its income (Knowles, 2003).

Developing Scholars at Howard Middle

Howard Middle School, in a high-income suburban community in southern Maine, is representative of the wealthier portion of the state. The school and district are well-funded and educational efforts are firmly supported by the children's parents, a high percentage of whom are professionals. The community's median household income was more than $58,000 in 2000, a figure some 56% higher than the state average.

Howard Middle is known to have one of the more successful laptop programs in the state, and both visitors and researchers are often pointed in its direction. Our observations and interviews at the school confirmed the success of the laptop program, and also pointed to how that success is intimately tied to the broader values, goals, and organization of the school. Simply put, Howard is a school dedicated to promoting academic expertise and research skills, and the use of laptops is geared toward this end. The overall academic direction of Howard was made very evident from our discussion with a school counselor, who explained that a serious career counseling initiative begins when students are in the fifth grade, and continues throughout all 4 years of the Grade 5–8 school. When we expressed surprise at how thorough the career counseling was for such a young age, the counselor explained that if fifth and sixth graders want to eventually get their master's or doctorate degrees, they need to start planning early. It was the first and only occasion that I had ever heard a school counselor discuss preparing fifth graders to take on doctoral work.

Starting Young. Howard students' training in information literacy also begins in the fifth grade, even though they don't enter the laptop program until 2 years later. All fifth graders attend a 45-minute weekly training session led by the librarian, Ms. Gompers, a highly accomplished professional who has two masters' degrees and a quarter century of educational experience and who had earlier won the statewide School Library Media Specialist of the Year award. She takes the students through a detailed process of how to search for information, starting with the school's electronic catalogues and proceeding through other electronic and print resources such as reference books and periodical indexes. Ms. Gompers explained to me her approach to information literacy:

> I'm teaching them about keywords and we were using a printed encyclopedia as an example but we also have the online version, so I'm tying in the fact that for the skills that we are learning it doesn't matter if it is online or in print in your hand or on a CD. I'm teaching them that the traditional research skills still have value in this modern world where information comes in many different formats, print and nonprint. And then today, the lesson that we are doing is bringing it right down to their level, we are using phone books and using keywords to search in phone books to find information. I really wanted to emphasize today that it is the process not the product that we are concerned with. The process is learning how to access information, and all these research tools that we have used are teaching them how to use them right now with the librarian right here. But when they get to be adults, and even at home in the afternoon without a teacher or librarian beside them, they may have a need for information and the skills that we are teaching them is transferable to "everyday life," and so we were using a phone book. Next week we are going to be looking at using keywords on the Internet, in search engines and directories. After April vacation, when they come back we are going

to do a big research project on a famous American. And they are going to have a chance to use all those skills that we have been working on.

Finding, Citing, and Evaluating Online Sources. Ms. Gompers has developed special bibliography forms with places for students to write down the citation for their sources (with an example of a correctly formatted citation at the top of the form), the search keywords they had used, and the students' notes on the information found. We regularly found students using these forms for their research, whether done from print sources in the library or from online sources using their laptops.

Ms. Gompers has also put considerable time and effort into assembling online academic resources and teaching students how to use them. The school subscribes to Grolier online, which offers three distinct encyclopedias, as well as World Book online. In addition, all schools in Maine have access to a suite of 25 online databases, including magazines, newspapers, reference works, biographies, radio and television transcripts, and primary source documents, from EBSCO information services.

Unlike other schools we visited, where students most frequently used general Internet searches for their research (e.g., Google, Yahoo, or Ask Jeeves), at Howard students tended to prefer more academic sources for their online information. As one student told us, in a fairly typical comment, explaining why she prefers to use the encyclopedia, "Well sometimes on Google, you don't really know where the sources are coming from and you don't know if they are accurate and trustworthy."

These critical views toward unknown sources are nurtured early on at Howard, again, long before students get their laptops. Ms. Gompers related an example of her work with a sixth-grade student at the library:

> Last year, I had a student who was doing rain forest research
> and went to Google and Googled her animal or bird, and then,
> unfortunately, she hadn't done what I asked students to do and
> that is immediately do your bibliography on her note paper.
> So it is time to pull all the pieces together and she's got notes
> hanging out there that she doesn't have a bibliography written
> so she comes to me and she asks me to help her with it. So of
> course I did. So we sat down and when we got to the site that
> we used, I realized that this site had been made by a student
> somewhere else in the country and I asked her if she had evalu-

ated this site. And she said, "Uh no, I didn't do that." So we sat down and looked at the site and we looked for the author and looked for the credentials and tried to find out why it was created and so on. And as we went down through the questions, she said to me, "I don't think this is such a good site." And I said, "You are absolutely right." Now there may be good information here but we have no idea how careful this student was, and we don't know why this student was an expert to put it out there on the web. So we went back and we found some other sites connected through an encyclopedia.

Howard is a school with a strong degree of parental involvement, as evidenced by the numerous parent volunteers we witnessed during our visits. To further involve parents in supporting their children's information literacy, Ms. Gompers organizes evening programs for parents, at which she introduces the online materials available through the encyclopedia subscriptions and EBSCO database and encourages parents to make use of them for their own needs, for example, to consult with *Consumer Reports* magazine before making purchases.

Working Across the Curriculum. Technology-enhanced research at Howard goes far beyond finding and critically evaluating online information. Rather, these discrete information literacy skills are part of a broader process of critical inquiry that begins when students enter the school in the fifth grade and extends from there. By the time students enter the one-to-one laptop program in the seventh grade, they are making use of the computer and the Internet for highly interactive forms of learning, as they work individually and in groups to define questions or problems, gather and analyze information and data, and develop high-quality products to present their findings. This took place in each of the main subject areas and also in interdisciplinary projects that were organized across subjects.

For example, to better understand the U.S. Constitution in social studies class, students visited the website of the Bill of Rights Institute, where they found information on recent court cases involving key constitutional issues. Students perused the site and selected cases of interest to them, which often involved issues of relevance to youth. For example, some students selected the case involving an atheist's challenge to the Pledge of Allegiance, and others chose a case involving a student's use of his camera phone to take and share embarrassing pictures of other students without their knowledge or permission. The students then read both their case and the background information on it, developed an opinion about the case, and wrote an essay of their opinion, which they emailed to the teacher. They then shared and debated their opinions in class. This represents a very different approach to the Constitution from that typically found in schools where students focus their effort on memorizing key facts and information (e.g., content of Constitution and its amendments, names of signers, historical dates). In contrast, the Bill of Rights activity described above forces students to grapple with the meaning of the Constitution and its applicability in today's world.

Students in mathematics classes carried out stock market projects, in which they selected and researched companies, simulated investments in stock, developed spreadsheets to track their earnings, and wrote reports incorporating their research and data analysis. The teacher had attempted similar projects in the past, but could not incorporate student research on companies as the information simply wasn't available in the school library. Now students are able to carry out and incorporate research on companies, as well as track stocks in real time. The math teacher explained to me the importance of this real-time information:

> If they need to get research, they can access it wherever they are. A teacher in the classroom says, "I wonder if something big happened in Iraq yesterday. I wonder what that did with the stock." We open [the laptops] up; we're on the stock market page. It's immediate, anytime, anywhere learning, access to data and information, whenever you want it. Say, "Alright, you guys go over and write." These guys are going to do some research. We're going to be doing spreadsheets and graphing. The tool's there whenever they need it.

Once a year, an entire grade level at Howard comes together for a broad interdisciplinary collaborative project. During our visits to the school, the seventh-grade students were working on a major project investigating the industrial revolution and examining the concept of progress, as it applied in four areas: Western expansion, technological progress, women's rights, and slavery. Students worked within one of these four areas developing both an essay and a multimedia presentation on their particular subtopic and how it relates to the overall theme of progress. For example, one student we observed and interviewed was investigating the history of railroads in the United States and the particular ways that they contributed to or hindered social, economic, and technological progress. As with all essays at the school, a detailed bibliography with citation of scholarly sources was required. The multimedia presentations included posters, skits, slide presentations, videos, and games, and were presented to parents and the community at a special evening show.

Lack of Direction at Plum High

Not all schools we visited were as successful as Howard Middle in promoting research skills with technology; a less successful laptop program was found at Plum High School. Plum is located in one of the most sparsely populated rural counties in Maine, with a median household income of less than $28,000, which is just 75% of the state average and less than half that of Howard Middle's community. Nevertheless, Plum was one of the first high schools in the state to implement a one-to-one laptop program when the owners of a local mill gave a large grant to the school for equipment. Interviews with the mill spokesperson and others in the community suggest a variety of possible motives for the grant: revitalizing the local economy; developing a more trained workforce; returning a favor to the governor (who was at the time promoting the laptop program) for facilitating permits and licenses for the mill.

On our visits to Plum we quickly learned that the school had a very different academic climate than that of Howard. Whereas Howard's walls featured posters promoting critical thinking, Plum's walls were adorned with military recruitment posters. One wall display indicating the plans of 12th graders revealed that only half the students who had entered the school 3 years' previously remained until graduation, and a large percentage of those were entering the armed forces. The counselors' office indicated it had no formal career counseling program and instead devoted much of its efforts to handling disciplinary problems, which had increased since the launching of the laptop program.

At the school library, we learned that there was no information literacy program at the library and that few of the students or teachers at the school were aware of the state-subscribed online databases available. Our classroom observations and interviews confirmed an indifferent approach to online research at Plum. Most students chose Google as their only instrument of online research and cited miscellaneous websites rather than more authoritative sources in print or online. Plum teachers, however, viewed their students' web citations as a sign of digital sophistication.

Although teachers at Plum assigned research projects, the learning processes and outcomes were dramatically different from those at

Howard. For example, a typical social studies research project at Plum that we had the opportunity to observe in detail involved students developing and presenting PowerPoint presentations on particular U.S. subcultures, such as the Apache Indians, the Amish, the homeless, cowboys, or Latinos. Since students were neither provided with nor asked to develop any research questions as they worked on this task, most students simply surfed the web to quickly gather information, often highly stereotypic, which they then cut and pasted into their PowerPoint presentations. The rest of the time was spent finding and inserting clip art or photos—again, usually stereotypic of the subculture—and embellishing their presentation with glitzy but purposeless transitions and backgrounds. A typical presentation contained eight slides, each with different backgrounds, fonts, and colors, but with virtually no original text; the content of the slides was lightly revised text from an online fact sheet, accompanied by stereotypical photos. The students then went to the front of the class one by one to deliver their presentations. Facing the screen rather than their audience, the students read out loud the material that they had just cut and pasted. Most other students paid little attention to the presentations, as they either continued working on their own PowerPoint presentations or occupied themselves with surfing the Web or instant messaging their friends.

Of course not all lessons at Plum were as disappointing as this one; in fact, I have already included some of the more positive examples from the school in Chapter 4 on writing. But, unfortunately, the general approach to information and research noted in this class was consistent with what we observed elsewhere in the school. Information literacy, especially the skills of evaluating and integrating information that is accessed, was not being taught.

From our perspective, a couple of factors explained the differences in research climate at Howard and Plum. The greater wealth of the Howard community and school district, as well as the desirable suburban location, meant that the district could have its pick of many of the state's best teachers and administrators. Plum, however, due to its location and depressed local economy, had difficulty even filling all of its teaching positions. Also at Howard, high academic expectations from parents (themselves largely professionals) kept the administration and staff on their toes, a factor that was less evident at Plum.

What is important, though, is not so much the distinction between these two schools, but the broader trends they represent. For schools that are already dedicated to promoting critical thinking and inquiry, laptops will prove to be an especially powerful learning tool. Schools without that orientation will not magically transform themselves merely through the use of laptops. It takes more than computers and Internet access to connect students to real learning opportunities.

Expeditionary Learning at Castle Middle

The third Maine school we visited, Castle Middle School, represents a fascinating alternative to both Howard and Plum, and indeed to any other school in Maine, in both its demographics and teaching approach.

Castle is located in one of the main cities in southern Maine. It serves the most ethnically, linguistically, and economically diverse population of any school district in Maine. About 25% of its students are African, Asian, Middle Eastern, or Latin American refugees and immigrants from working-class neighborhoods; some 17 countries and 28 languages are represented among the school's small population. About 50% of its students are White youth from some of the most destitute housing projects of the eastern seaboard. And about 25% of its students are middle- or upper-middle-class students from other surrounding neighborhoods. As a highly diverse school within one of Maine's wealthier southern counties, it thus falls outside the state's traditional north–south categories.

In the school's earlier years, the kind of inequality described above between Howard and Plum was reproduced within Castle's walls, with seven distinct educational tracks, including one for the highly gifted, one for the accelerated (but not gifted), one for special education, one for non-English speakers, and several others calibrated by ability. A new principal was hired who had a mission of promoting an equal and quality education for all Castle students. The principal, Mr. Miller, turned to a national pilot program developed by Outward Bound, and in 1992 Castle Middle became one of nine Expeditionary Learning Outward Bound schools (for information on the history, learning principles, and practices of this movement, see Expeditionary Learning, 2006). The Expeditionary Learning program involved a complete remaking of the school and curriculum. Tracking ended, and students from special education and ESL programs were integrated into regular classrooms to the maximum extent possible. All students were grouped into "houses" of about 60 learners and four main teachers, with the teachers in each house having broad autonomy over class scheduling. Most houses developed highly flexible block scheduling, with classes meeting for different lengths of time on different days and ample time built in for teacher collaboration. Most important, almost all academic work in the houses and school was integrated into 8- to 12-week interdisciplinary research projects. These projects, or "learning expeditions," are designed to break with what Mr. Miller called "the tyranny of coverage of curriculum," and instead involve students in collaborative inquiry on thematic issues. These learning expeditions are somewhat similar to the Howard project described above (on the topic of progress), except there are two or more of these projects a year at Castle and they thus comprise the majority of the school curriculum.

In the mid- to late-1990s, the Expeditionary Learning model evolved, as the school's technology coordinator and classroom teachers worked to make new media central to many areas of learning, with students using computers, the Internet, and other digital media to carry out inquiry and develop products. Later, the school issued laptops to all students in the seventh grade (2002) and eighth grade (2003), and one-to-one computing further supported students' research. Students use laptops to gather data and information on their research topics, write up their investigations, and produce multimedia products on their findings incorporating texts, images, sounds, and video.

For example, in one recent learning expedition, Fading Footprints, students collaboratively investigated how diversity strengthens an ecosystem (see details of this project in Grant, n.d.). Each participating student produced a species page incorporating factual information, an essay, and artwork on a different endangered species. This work, along with 25 concept pages on related topics such as diversity, extinction, and the Endangered Species Act, was incorporated into a CD-ROM. Another expedition, One Nation/Divided Lives, addressed a series of major questions related to the U.S. Civil War, including why people go to war; how the Civil War affected groups, families, and individuals; and how the Civil War affected the United States as a nation.

Almost all of the learning expeditions at Castle result in collaborative multimedia creations (we will consider that aspect of this work—the design and production of media—in Chapter 6), but here the point is to consider how such overall projects framed and supported students' development of information literacy and research skills. To see how this is accomplished, a comparison to the research project at Plum High on subcultures is informative. In both cases, students investigated particular subtopics within a broader theme: At Plum each student chose a different subculture whereas at Castle, each student in the Fading Footprints project selected a species. At Castle, however, students were able to situate their own research within broader research questions. Together with the facts that they gathered about their species (on topics such as habitat, present status, diet and feeding habits, and causes of endangerment), Castle students also had to write an essay relating their own findings to the overall research question of how diversity strengthens an ecosystem. The essays were of varying quality, reflecting the comparatively limited language and literacy skills of many Castle students; nevertheless, writing an interpretive essay distinguished this type of project from merely collecting facts such as in the subculture assignments carried out at Plum. Castle students who completed their species pages ahead of their peers went on to produce concept pages containing more in-depth conceptual work. All of the students were then required to read each of the 25 concept pages and to insert hyperlinks in their own work to several key concepts from the concept pages. This once again helped students connect their own fact-finding to broader concepts and ideas. Finally, students at Castle were provided scaffolding for their work through detailed peer editing during a "critique week" with the assistance of teacher-supplied rubrics.

Castle thus represents a radical break with traditional curriculum in favor of inquiry-based and project-based learning. In California and elsewhere, many teachers and schools shy away from such approaches believing that they might negatively affect student test scores. Interestingly though, Castle's combined test scores in reading, writing, mathematics, and science have exceeded the state average in Maine in 2004–05, as they have for a number of years, in spite of the school's large numbers of non-native speakers of English and low-income students. Castle has thus shown that project-based learning and intensive technology use can be combined for academic success with diverse students.

CONCLUSION

Widely valued twenty-first-century learning skills revolve around working with information to produce knowledge. Our investigation in the 10 schools of our project illustrated the decided advantage that the laptop classroom has for facilitating these kinds of skills. Learning in laptop classes had more frequent opportunities for just-in-time learning, individualized learning, and empirical investigation. Laptop use made it much more feasible for students to engage in research projects and also created better possibilities for in-depth learning.

However, these beneficial outcomes occurred unevenly in the schools we visited. Though all students had frequent access to information, not all received the instruction and scaffolding necessary to develop information literacy and research skills. In particular, teachers in high-income communities were more likely to expect and promote critical inquiry and information literacy than were teachers in low-income areas. This discrepancy is consistent with previous research on technology use in non-laptop schools, which has similarly found more promotion of higher order thinking skills with technology in high-SES than in low-SES schools (see, for example, Becker, 2000b; Schofield & Davidson, 2004; Warschauer, 2000a; Warschauer, Knobel, et al., 2004; Wenglinsky, 1998). To a certain extent, this is a reflection of the broader socioeconomic context of today's world and the social sorting mechanism of U.S. schools (see Kozol, 2005). Though most workers will require some information technology skills to function in tomorrow's workforce, those skills are bifurcated between knowl-edge-producing functions (e.g., analysis, interpretation, research) and administrative functions (Net browsing, basic communication, and file maintenance; see discussion in Castells, 1999; Gee, Hull, & Lank-shear, 1996; Warschauer, 2000a). It is thus not surprising that schools that see themselves producing the academic and business elite tend to emphasize the former set of skills, and that schools that see them-selves as preparing students vocationally tend to emphasize the latter.

However, our research in laptop schools suggests that these pat-terns are not set in stone. Though socioeconomic context is an impor-tant variable, vision, values, and beliefs are also crucial factors. Those schools that have a vision for promoting information literacy and re-search skills with diverse students, and that can mobilize their teach-ers behind that vision, are finding one-to-one laptops a powerful tool toward this goal.

CHAPTER 6

Media and Design

What we really try to focus on is saying, "what are you going to make at the end of the day that can include everybody's work in it, that becomes a socially constructing environment of knowledge that everybody's trying to put together?" The laptops, to the extent that we are doing this well, allow kids to produce information in a variety of ways and media. So we get this big, broad canvas for catching a lot of different stuff, and if we're smart, we don't just represent it once and publish it and make it finished product, but we take all that stuff and we create a social environment, where everybody looks at each other's work and has a chance to comment on, add to, or connect to what each person's saying. And so socially we construct this picture of a curriculum, and then after a round of that, we might publish. It shows kids that you begin something, you work on it for a while, you do some editing, but eventually you show us what you learn. And I think with the laptops, we're in the process of getting to a place where they can really blow the lid off the traditional way of doing the work because it takes away a lot of limitations.

—Media specialist teacher, Castle Middle School

From the fifteenth to twentieth centuries, printed texts reigned supreme in mass communication. However, this supremacy steadily eroded with advances in photography, radio, film, and television. The development and diffusion of personal computers, game consoles, and the Internet brought forth entirely new forms of interaction and communication that incorporated images, sounds, and video. The more recent spread of wireless networks and next-generation digital devices— including digital cameras, digital camcorders, digital video recorders, digital video projectors, and portable media players—means that the typographic era is essentially over, replaced by a new era of multimodal communication. This is a positive development, in that audiovisual material, when compared to print, is both richer in content and more easily understood by people based on our evolutionary history of responding to things we see and hear in the environment (Bolter, 1991; Kaplan, 1995).

The emergence of a posttypographic era does not mean that written texts will disappear, but just that they will continue to evolve within a broader and richer communicative landscape. For example, Kress (1998) documents how print genres themselves have radically changed in the last few decades, with images, figures, and diagrams now playing a much more central role in everything from newspapers to science textbooks. Typographical literacy will remain enormously important, but the ways that people read and write will change (see discussion in Chapters 3 and 4), and new forms of meaning making with multimedia will be increasingly valued.

Similar changes in literacy have occurred throughout history following the emergence of other major technologies of communication. The development of writing undermined the oral literacies of reciting and listening to epic poetry (Ong, 1982). Later, the spread of the printing press undermined the literacies involved in copying or reading aloud manuscripts, while making possible new forms of literacy involved in studying published texts (Eisenstein, 1979). The current rise of information and communication technologies will likely have a similarly large impact on literacy practices.

REPRESENTING KNOWLEDGE IN MULTIPLE MEDIA

There is broad recognition that schools need to better integrate multimedia in education (e.g., see North Central Regional Educational Laboratory & The Metiri Group, 2003). There are three important reasons to introduce multimedia production in schools: multimedia literacy, knowledge representation, and student engagement. *Multimedia literacy* refers to the set of skills required to interpret and create products or messages that make use of images, photographs, video, animation, music, sounds, and typography. Among other things, it includes an understanding of frame composition; color palette; audio, image, and video editing techniques; sound-text-image relations; the effects of typography; transitional effects; navigation and interface construction; and generic conventions in diverse media (Daley, 2003). In the twenty-first century, multimedia literacy is important for occupational purposes (with an increasing amount of jobs requiring production of multimodal content), civic purposes (with full participation in society enhanced by the ability to interpret and produce multimedia through blogging, podcasting, website creation, and so on), and artistic purposes (with digital photography, digital video, and other forms of new media emerging as important forms of art and self-expression).

Knowledge representation refers to the power of multimedia for organizing, interpreting, and construing experience and information. Subject teachers in a variety of areas are interested in having their students interact with and create multimedia not only for the general literacy skills developed, but more important, for the academic content knowledge gained in the process as students deploy the added power of images, sound, and video in their efforts to develop and represent their knowledge.

The third important reason is to enhance student engagement. The millennial and postmillennial generations are growing up as natives of the multimodal era. For many students, game boxes, iPods, digital cameras, wireless laptops, and camera-equipped cell phones are the norm, and they are immersed in accessing, interacting with, and creating multimedia throughout the day and night (see Lenhart & Madden, 2005). They expect to continue such types of media-rich learning in school. Of course, not all families can afford this range of equipment, but students without this home access usually find the opportunity to engage with new media in school even more compelling (e.g., see Velastegui, 2005). In other words, there has been a broad cultural shift in how children prefer to learn that affects learners from diverse backgrounds. Engagement, however, is a two-edged sword, as students' excitement of working with multimedia, if not handled well, can be a distraction from attention to underlying academic content.

For the most part, schools have not been very successful at integrating multimedia in instruction (see discussion in Warschauer, Knobel et al., 2004). Except in one-to-one classrooms, the challenge of scheduling shared computer labs or mobile laptop carts means that educational use of multimedia often becomes an add-on, rather than being naturally integrated into course content. Students in typical classrooms use digital media infrequently enough that they seldom have opportunities to develop advanced multimedia literacy, but focus instead on the basics of how to operate the software. Specialized courses in video production or digital photography that develop more advanced meaning-making or artistic skills are accessible only to a small portion of students. The lack of opportunity to work with new media is thus a factor contributing to student disengagement from school.

In contrast, in the laptop schools we visited in this study, students worked extensively with digital media on a daily basis. The integration of media access and production into instruction occurred naturally, thus providing students a wider array of tools for knowledge representation and construction. Students developed greater meaning-making, communication, and artistic skills with new media, and they found their work with new media highly engaging.

In this chapter, I examine six key concepts related to multimedia use in education and discuss how these concepts were realized or addressed in the laptop classroom.

RESEMIOTIZATION

Iedema (2001, 2003) uses the term *resemiotization* to describe the shifting of communicative or interpretive material across meaning-making modes, for example, taking textual material and expressing it through an image. Others describe this process as *transduction* (Kress, 2003) or *mode switching* (Baynham, 1993). Whatever the term used, it is clear that the repurposing of information across modes is enormously important in both society and schools. Such resemiotization is critical to the work that symbolic analysts do as they constantly interpret and analyze information and content and reshape messages into alternate media. In education, such mode switching allows learners to take a fresh look at a message and explore it from an alternate lens.

This kind of resemiotization occurred constantly in the laptop classrooms as students drew on a wide range of multimedia resources to shift analytic and interpretive modes. We illustrate this through two examples from the study of literature. In both cases, students drew on modalities and media that are highly influential in youth culture but until now have been largely absent from the classroom.

In the first example, a teacher at Nancy Middle School in California had her students develop a literary newspaper to explore the themes of Beowulf (see also Chapter 2). This allowed the students to tackle a highly abstract medieval poem and interpret it within a more familiar genre or collection of genres, one of which was the comic strip. Today's youth are highly interested in comics, not only as readers (for example, of Japanese manga; see discussion in Black, in press) but also as authors, as witnessed by the huge number of graphic novels published online (see discussion in Pearce, 2002). By including a comic strip within a broader constellation of interpretive assignments, the instructor gave students a chance for a highly creative resemiotization.

Figure 6.1 shows one student's artful comic-book rendering of the two major battles of the poem, as Beowulf confronts the monster Grendel, and the dragon Firedrake. The student's visual rendering of the violence accentuates the thematic links between the brutality of the fights and Beowulf's heroic nature and his boldness. The left-right frame sequencing of the comic offers movement to the plot without the need to encode it linguistically. The climax of each fight scene

Figure 6.1. Comic Interpretation of Beowulf

builds up through the penultimate frame, and the tension is then re-leased in the final frame, a convention typical in many Westernized comics. Language in this comic sequence does not need to function as the primary means of summary. Instead, it can be used to imbue the characters with personality. Thus we see Beowulf as a warrior with a dry sense of humour who holds up the arm he has just ripped off of Grendel and muses about its effectiveness as a souvenir and a back-scratcher. Beowulf is also shown to have a heroic flaw, cast as someone who, despite 50 years of peace for his people, is ready for some action, claiming, "I'm bored" as a set-up for his final battle. Through the af-fordances of mixing the visual and written in this multimodal comic sequence, the student imposes his own imagined world onto the repre-sentational frame offered by the Beowulf narrative.

An equally interesting, and more widespread, example of resemio-tization took place through musical interpretation of literature. We were particularly surprised by the inclusion of musical composition in several California schools that we visited in 2004–05, as none of the Maine schools we observed the prior year had included this as a feature of language arts instruction. This was due to the fact that Ap-ple's GarageBand software was included in the iBooks purchased in

2004–05, but not in the year earlier, and illustrated how fast media use in and out of schools is changing. Language arts teachers quickly found ways to exploit the software by having students compose pieces that illustrated prose or poetry they had read. For example, in one typical assignment, students at Henry Elementary in California used Apple's iPhoto and GarageBand software to set the mood for part of the poem "The Midnight Ride of Paul Revere," with an image and brief musical interlude. The teacher of the class—widely regarded as one of the best teachers in the school district because of both her high academic standards and her creative use of educational technology—explained how this type of project helped her gifted students develop their analytic skills:

> They had to get the emotion, the tone, the climax of the poem.
> They had to be very thoughtful and think rhetorically. It wasn't
> a matter of "this was the answer to the question," but "what
> was the emotion going on in the poem?" They thought more
> deeply about the poem.

HYBRIDITY

The concept of *hybridity* (Fairclough, 1992a; 1992b; New London Group, 1996; Ware & Warschauer, in press) shares much in common with resemiotization, in that it also often entails a change of modalities. However, hybridity suggests not so much a shifting of modes, but rather a creative mixing of modes, media, genres, formats, and dialects, for example, by writing an academic paper as an online, illustrated hypertext. Such hybridity occurs constantly outside of school, especially in youth-oriented digital media environments (see discussion in Lam, 2005; Luke, 2003). However, it is not typically favored in schools, which tend to stick to the tried and true, especially in the face of high-stakes standards and assessments.

This is unfortunate, as hybridity serves valuable learning purposes. It provides a way to actively engage learners in meaning making by allowing them to creatively draw on a range of semiotic resources. It also allows students an opportunity to bridge the gap between the types of academic literacy required in school—valuable but often inaccessible—and the ways of communicating more familiar to their lives, thus tapping students' funds of knowledge (Gonzales et al., 2005).

In the laptop schools, we witnessed students and teachers enthusiastically embracing hybrid forms as a way to help make learning more meaningful for students. One particularly illustrative example of this occurred in a science class at Nancy Junior High in California, where teachers are constantly seeking ways to better reach the low-SES Latino students who make up the majority of the student population. The teacher of the class, Ms. Larson, had high academic standards for her students, but was also highly flexible in terms of how those standards were achieved. In this particular unit students were invited to write a narrative of any sort that demonstrated their understanding of the terms, concepts, and processes of the human nervous system. The majority of students wrote stories whose words, typography, and images served to combine an academic description of cell structure with popular culture. For example, a multimedia composition by Susan drew on her interest in the popular hip-hop artists, Usher and Chili. Drawing on both the romance stories of music stars and the core science text, Susan explored academic knowledge of human impulse control by applying it to a real-world scenario of heartbreak and deceit. In the text, written from a third-person perspective and dedicated "to all the broken hearts," Susan chronicled a fictitious account of the real-life breakup between Usher and Chili. Her narrative depicted Chili as a strong female character whose teacher assigned her work on a project on the nervous system with her slacker boyfriend Usher. There were a number of jabs that Chili made against her soon-to-be-ex boyfriend Usher, who had cheated on her, and each of these was tied to the display of factual knowledge about the nervous system. Thus in an accusation against Usher's fidelity, Susan linked Chili's attack on her boyfriend to the somatic system, which "deals with actions that you control, kind of like when you cheat on your girlfriend—don't you control that, Usher?" But Usher, who was confused, skipped ahead to "the automatic system [which] deals with action that you don't control, like when you have those sudden urges to maybe be with another girl."

The final product was illustrated with images of Usher and Chili clipped and pasted off the Internet and packaged onto colorful pages of construction paper. In this text, the affordances of the graphic images served not to move the narrative forward, but rather to display personally relevant cultural icons as an integral part of a school-based text. The personalization of abstract principles of the somatic and automatic systems allowed Susan to depict Chili as a strong character in charge of her learning, even in the face of humiliation by her ex-boyfriend. She was the one who studied for exams, produced quality work, and had self-awareness of her learning: "So Chili told Usher to start outlining his thoughts and Usher said 'What thoughts?'" By weaving in science facts, the hybrid text transcended the mere reproduction of a typical romance narrative, and by situating the academic task of knowledge display within a battle of wills between two lovers, it served as a vehicle for the student to align herself with the female protagonist who triumphed not through love, at least in this case, but through the power of knowledge.

Most important, from the teacher's point of view, the narrative undoubtedly helped Susan cement her knowledge of the nervous system. By taking the unfamiliar (biology) and reframing it in terms of the familiar (popular culture), Susan deployed a learning strategy that has long been known to be effective for mastering new material (see Ausubel, 1960).

PERSUASION

The notion of *persuasion* has a special place in media education. Prior to the current emphasis on *multimedia literacy*, which focuses on students as media *producers*, there has been an earlier emphasis on *media literacy*, which focuses on students as media *consumers*. Proponents of media literacy seek to promote a critical understanding of mass media's role in society, particularly in regard to the persuasive role of media in areas such as advertising, marketing, and politics. Similarly, those who approach multimedia literacy from an occupational training perspective often focus on the persuasive role of new media, as seen for example by the ubiquitous use of PowerPoint presentations in executive sales pitches.

In the laptop schools we visited, students were commonly assigned to critique persuasive use of media and to develop their own multimedia that debunked false claims. For example, students at Nancy Junior High used a public health website to examine tobacco advertisements aimed at youth (Campaign for Tobacco-Free Kids, 2006). They then created multimedia posters that included examples of the advertisements, highlighted their claims and messages, and counterposed them with facts about the tobacco industry and the effects of smoking.

In many classes, students went beyond critiquing advertisements to developing their own advertisements or promotional pieces. For example, students in a health class at Howard Middle School in Maine analyzed five fad diets and then produced their own video infomercial advertising a new fad diet they created. Students at Nancy Junior High produced a brief video public service announcement on Internet safety for children. Students in a social studies class at Castle Middle School in Maine developed slide presentations explaining why a particular African country was a good candidate to host the Olympics. Third- and fourth-grade students at Henry Elementary in California developed a brief video commercial inviting tourists to a particular planet.

It seemed to us that working on these promotional pieces had several benefits for students. First, as in the projects discussed above under resemiotization and hybridization, students were able to internalize content by translating it to a mode (e.g., video) and a genre (e.g., advertisements) that they were familiar with. Yet while students have witnessed thousands of ads in their lifetime, they have probably not often thought critically about the medium. By actually developing advertisements or promotional pieces themselves, they gained greater awareness of how multimedia is used to convey a message. They also were forced to think analytically about their topic (e.g., what aspects of an African country's geography, demographics, economy, culture, and society would make it suitable to host a major international sports event) rather than merely reporting on it (e.g., a paper or PowerPoint presentation providing an overview of an African country). They also developed some design skills in new media, though that issue will be discussed more in the next two sections on genre and design.

GENRE

The role of *genre* in composition instruction has long been controversial (see debates in Reid, 1987). On the one hand, an overly stringent focus on genre can hamper student creativity, discourage attention to writing process, and result in stilted five-paragraph essays. On the other hand, insufficient attention to academic genres can leave students adept at personal expression but without an understanding of the structure of academic writing.

The stakes are especially high, regarding whether and how to include genre in instruction, for low-SES students, English-language learners, and other at-risk students who may lack out-of-school experience with academic language and academic texts. Students on the margins need to find the power of their own voices if they are to see school as meaningful to their own lives. Yet they also need explicit attention to genre if they are to access the "voices of power," that is, the ways of writing and communicating that bring people academic success (Auerbach, 1997, p. 1).

When multimedia is thrown into the mix, the role of genre becomes that much more complex, as multimodal genres are in a state of rapid flux. However, as Kress (2003) points out, generic forms of any type are not a stable and idealized type, but rather a form of conventionalized social action, a way an actor seeks to get a message across by framing a text, product, or activity according to certain norms to accomplish a purpose. All genres are thus inherently unstable and impure; consider, for example, how the genre of the novel has changed over time and how much variation such a genre includes.

Effective approaches to teaching multimodal genres adopt the same principles for teaching written genre suggested by Auerbach (1997): to seek to allow students access to the voices of power while also allowing them to find the power of their own voice. This can be accomplished by merging the strengths of the genre and process approaches to composition. This involves showing students actual and multiple exemplars of the genre at hand (rather than idealized forms); drawing students' attention to the way that authors make choices (in both content and form) to accomplish their purposes within a genre; and then providing students plenty of opportunity to plan, compose, and edit their work while receiving critical feedback from peers and the instructor (Badger & White, 2000; Martin, Christie, & Rothery 1994).

Such approaches to teaching multimodal composition are rarely found in the typical classroom. Instead, you are more likely to find instruction such as we noted in a previous research project, in which a teacher assigned maximum grades for PowerPoint presentations based on how many fonts, sounds, slide transition types, and animations his student used, rather than on their achievement of any communicative purpose (Warschauer, Knobel, & Stone et al., 2004). The exception to this rule is the specialized media production course, such as video production or digital photography. These courses, both in typical and laptop schools, are often taught by people with more specialized media skills and thus include more sophisticated approaches to developing multimedia literacy and understanding multimodal genres. However, in a typical school, these courses are taught in a special laboratory and are thus available only to handful of students. In contrast, the laptop schools we visited were able to make such instruction available to a much larger number of students.

I will discuss three examples of genre-focused instruction in the laptop schools, one within a language arts classroom and two within specialized elective classes.

Movie Trailers at Nancy Junior High

Among academic subject teachers, we noted that language arts instructors were generally more attuned than others to issues of genre, composition principles, and literacy in multimodal realms. This is likely due to their overall focus on effective communication, as opposed, for example, to science and math teachers, who often see their focus as more limited to subject area content. A number of the language arts teachers we observed paid special attention in their instruction to the principles of effective communication in slide presentations, or to teaching how certain combinations of colors and shapes more effectively demonstrated an organizational plan while using a graphic organizer, or how certain types of clip art did or did not contribute to a message.

Sometimes teachers went beyond these general points of effective multimedia use to explicitly teach certain genres. An excellent example of this is the movie trailer project in Ms. Patterson's class at Nancy Junior High. The project, briefly mentioned in Chapter 2, involved the collaborative production of a movie trailer to advertise an imaginary film based on a novel students had read in class. To prepare for the task, students first visited two Internet sites of movie trailers (Apple Computer, 2005; Yahoo! Movies, 2005) and one site about digital storytelling (Center for Digital Storytelling, 2005). Making use of a detailed handout developed by the teacher, they analyzed sample material on the sites, considering what techniques might be useful to their own movie trailer, and then analyzed the book to consider how its scenes, narrative, and characters could best be summarized for the trailer they were creating. A storyboard planning sheet provided by the instructor provided further scaffolding for the students, including suggestions on the type of material that might go into the beginning, middle, and end of the trailer. Finally, the teacher-developed scoring rubric incorporated points for the trailer's content (scenes, narration, and characters), artistry (transitions, effects, music, sound effects, titles, and timing), and editing, thus helping promote the idea that both message and medium were important. Ongoing opportunities were built in for teams to receive feedback on their trailers from other teams and the instructor.

While the students were thus provided much scaffolding and support, they were also given a great deal of leeway to construct their trailer in ways that suited their own purpose, which varied depending on the points they chose to emphasize and the main targeted audience (children, teenagers, adults). Students took a great deal of pride in their products and shared them with tremendous enthusiasm, first with the whole class and then again with members of the research team. It was clear through the process that students had analyzed the book carefully and had considered how its message could be best summarized and communicated through a movie trailer. They also achieved the experience of creating a movie trailer and comparing their creation both to those of other students as well as to exemplars available online.

Digital Stories at Howard Middle School

The next two examples come from what are considered elective classes, but ones that are taken by all the students at the respective schools. This was part of a pattern in which specialized multimedia literacy instruction that is usually accessible only to some students in video production or digital photography classes at typical schools becomes a part of the regular curriculum at laptop schools.

For example, at Howard Middle School in Maine, all students take Industrial Arts. It is, by tradition, the school's "shop" course, and students carry out a number of hands-on projects with physical materials such as a bridge-building project discussed later in this chapter. However, the instructor, Mr. Morris has gradually integrated new technology into the instruction, both as a way of documenting student work with other materials (see example of wood bridges in "Reflection" section below) and also to teach technology use as a form of industrial art in itself. Students in the seventh grade learn to produce digital stories of their lives, whereas students in the eighth grade learn to produce original Claymations.

As with the movie trailer project discussed above, students start these projects by careful examination of authentic exemplars. For example, in the digital story assignment, they began by watching about a dozen other well-made digital stories. As they watched together, Mr. Morris pointed out artistic techniques related to transition types, titling, and other features. By examining these techniques in context, they were understood as contributing to certain artistic purposes, rather than merely for show. The students then brought in 40–70 personal pictures from their entire life, digitally photographed them for importation into their laptops, and used iMovie to compose their own digital stories. Once students had been exposed to various techniques, they were given full rein to decide which ones to use and how to achieve their desired ends, but Mr. Morris added suggestions and comments as students proceeded. The final products we watched showed appropriate attention to photograph selection, panning techniques, sequence, transition, and titling to communicate a personal story.

At the end the project is burned onto a videotape or DVD so that students can share it with their families. Interviews with students indicated that this was an enormously popular project that allowed them to gain valued artistic and technical skills while creating a moving portrayal of their life history.

Digital Photography at Flower School

The most ambitious program we observed for promotion of multimedia literacy took place at Flower School in California. As a brand new school with a science and technology focus, Flower offers only one middle school elective, technology. Over a 3-year period, the course covers a wide curriculum, including use of productivity software (word processing, spreadsheets, database management), digital photography, digital video production, Claymation, and robotics.

We visited the productivity software (sixth grade) and digital photography (seventh grade) classes on a number of occasions. Digital photography was taught similarly to a film photography class, with both technical instruction (e.g., use of tripod and camera, digital editing techniques such as cropping and sepia toning) and artistic instruction (e.g., the differences between close-up, medium, and long shots; the rule of thirds for photo composition). In both classes, all techniques taught were very soon deployed in creations of diverse genres, which included informational posters, Mother's Day Cards, book covers, CD covers, newspapers, and illustrated poems. As in the other classes discussed above, the use of techniques within purposeful and expressive creations helped students understand that such techniques serve communicative and artistic objectives.

In summary, most youth today get a great deal of experience in working with digital photographs and digitized music files outside of school, and some also work with digital video. But few have the understanding of technique, composition, and genre necessary to produce artistic posters, movie trailers, or digital stories. While none of these genres may be as important to students' academic futures as essay writing, we believe that their inclusion in the curriculum enriches students' lives in numerous ways. Mr. Morris commented, in reference to the significance of the digital story project for children and their families:

This really causes the kids to go through their scrapbooks and reflect on their life to date. The people that are most impressed with this are their parents and grandparents. I get so many comments from parents saying that they watched this video and cried, that we want a copy of this for the children's grand-parents. So this is touching their heart as much as their mind.

In general, we found much more attention to teaching multimodal genres in the laptop schools than in typical schools. This came largely from the more regular access to technology in the classroom, and consequently more curricular and pedagogical attention to how to make use of technology for diverse forms of meaning making.

REFLECTION

The foregoing comment by Mr. Morris points to another benefit of multimedia use in the laptop classroom: to enhance reflective learning. *Reflection* is a critical component of educational and human development, not only for the emotive aspects described above, but also for promoting analytic and critical thinking. For example, in Heath's (1983) classic ethnographic study of language use in three communities, she describes how middle-class parents foster reflective thinking and analysis among their children:

> It is as though in the drama of life, townspeople parents freeze scenes and parts of scenes at certain points along the way. Within the single frame of a scene, they focus the child's attention on objects or events in the frame, sort out referents for the child to name, give the child ordered turns for sharing talk about this referent, and then narrate a description of the scene. Through their focused language, adults make the potential stimuli in the child's environment stand still for a cooperative examination and narration between parent and child. The child learns to focus attention on a preselected referent, masters the relationships between the signifier and the signified, develops turn-taking skills in a focused conversation on the referent, and is subsequently expected to listen to, benefit from, and eventually to create narratives placing the referent in different contextual situations. (p. 351)

Historically, there have been limited means for freezing scenes for analysis. In Heath's example, such freezing is accomplished through immediate interaction at the time the event occurs. Portable digital cameras and camcorders, especially when combined with personal computers for archiving, reviewing, editing, or sharing digital files, magnify students' abilities to capture their experiences and use them for reflection. We witnessed many examples of student media use for documentation and analysis. The purpose of this was to allow students to reflect on their individual performance, their collaborative project work, and other people's actions and opinions.

Analyzing Student Performance

We witnessed several examples of student use of video to document and analyze their own performance. For example, in an Industrial Arts class at Howard Middle School, students designed and built model bridges out of wood. They then placed a brick on top of the bridge while videotaping. Most of the bridges could hold the brick, but for those that couldn't, a subsequent frame by frame analysis of how and where the bridge collapsed indicated to the students the precise flaws in their design.

Another example comes from foreign language instruction, which for the most part is notoriously ineffective in U.S. schools, especially in promoting oral language skills. Ms. Maxwell, a French teacher at Howard Middle School, found one approach to get students to focus more on oral language development. Students in her class perform 3–4 skits throughout the year incorporating the French vocabulary and themes they are studying in class, and the skits are videotaped by other students. The performers then view the videos and fill out a reflection sheet on their language use, looking in particular for language structures that have been the focus of instruction. As Maxwell explained,

> They watch themselves. And they write down "what can you work on next time?" whether they stood still too much or they kept making mistakes in their words, or they kept forgetting their lines, or, no matter how many times we kept saying it's *pizarra*, they kept on saying *pizarro*. So they had to really do a reflection of their work.

The videotaping of the skits not only allows for a means of reflection, but also motivates and engages students. "Sometimes the kids who are very, very quiet suddenly become very innovative," explained Maxwell. "They love the acting piece of it and they get into character."

Maxwell also requires the students to show the videotapes to their parents, which keeps the parents better informed about their students' progress and provides additional incentive for the students to do well. As Maxwell told us,

It's really the first time that the parents get to watch their children speak in the language because many times parents will say "let me hear you speak some French or Spanish" and the kids are like "ahhh," you know, "I don't want to say anything." But with the movies, and because they have to show their parents, it really gives their parents a chance to [see and hear them], and it's wonderful, the comments we get back from parents, the feedback has been great because they say "I didn't realize they could speak that well."

The students keep an archive of all the videotapes on their laptop throughout the year, and at the end of the year are asked to reflect on them again, which helps them better understand the progress they have made since the beginning of the year and encourages further improvement.

Documenting Project Work

Sometimes such media production is used not so much to analyze individual performance as to document student's collective work on major projects. This is especially the case at Castle Middle School, where almost all learning expeditions also include a video documentary component. Participation on the video documentary team is highly coveted, and students usually apply through submitting a résumé and cover letter (thus providing another literacy activity, as discussed in Chapter 3). They then document all aspects of the expedition, such as kick-off events, instructions or rules, formation of teams, visits from guest speakers, student fieldwork, research, product creation, assessment, and, when appropriate, competition.

We examined the videos produced for two expeditions, and they were highly creative, entertaining, and informative. For example, in one project called Junkyard Wars, students worked in teams to produce small robots that could grip, move, and put down different-size objects, with the robots competing against each other in a final competition. The student-produced video documentary on the project reviewed the rules and regulations of the competition, highlighted the design process of the different teams, demonstrated what materials the teams gathered and used, and showed both the testing of the robots and their performance in the final competition, all nicely edited and accompanied by appropriate music. The video, which was published on a CD, provided a memento for students of a major middle school project, informed parents about their student's educational activity, offered a resource for other educators who wish to organize similar projects, and served as a resource for this class and other classes to reflect back on what worked and didn't work in the robot design and competition.

Recording Others' Views

Access to digital cameras, laptop computers, and video editing software also allowed students to record the actions and words of others outside the classroom. Such video documentation was incorporated into a variety of subjects. For example, 11th-grade students at Melville High engaged in a semester-long project on twentieth-century history. Students worked in teams to explore a series of questions related to twentieth-century history, to develop and present a multimedia presentation on their topic, and to participate in a panel discussion on their topic. In addition to making the presentation and participating on the panel, they had to develop and submit a detailed bibliography and copies of key readings that helped them prepare for their presentation and panel.

As in many of the projects of this sort that we witnessed, students were given a great deal of autonomy as to what sorts of media to develop to support their presentation. The assignment was thus not "to make a PowerPoint," but rather to address certain research questions in a presentation using whatever media appear appropriate. This kind of student autonomy, common in laptop classrooms, contrasted to what we've witnessed in prior typical classrooms in which media assignments are usually technology driven rather than content driven.

In the presentation that we observed, a group of students was exploring the topic "the roots of evil," examining why and how evil emerges and what the responsibilities of the international community are to deal with it. They decided to develop a video on the topic, the centerpiece of which was interviews with people at the school and the community voicing their opinions on the nature of evil leaders, from Mussolini to Hitler to Saddam Hussein, and on the legitimacy of international actions taken to depose these regimes. The video allowed students to gather, edit, and critically examine the voices of the public to put forth competing perspectives on how evil regimes emerge and what should be done about them. The follow-up panel discussions demonstrated that students had explored the underlying questions in depth and were prepared to intelligently discuss the issues.

In summary, though these three types of video documentation differ, they all allow students to freeze scenes and reflect on them. The

French teacher, Ms. Maxwell, summarized the difference between teaching that included this kind of video recording of student work and prior teaching:

> Before they really couldn't do any kind of self-evaluation because they never saw themselves again. And what we're finding is that no matter how many times they play that movie back, they don't get tired of it. They play it over, and over, and over, and they edit it and add music or background. And each time, they pick up something. So in the past when we did skits, they really couldn't evaluate themselves and it was just me giving feedback to them. . .because sometimes they'll say "but I thought I said that?" And I say no. "But I thought I pronounced that right?" And I said no. And now, I can write those same things down and I say, "Now play the movie back." And they'll say, "You're right. I missed the word," or "I said the wrong word," or "I mispronounced it."

AUDIENCE

As discussed in Chapter 4, immature writers usually produce writer-based prose, rather than reader-based prose (Flower, 1984). The knowledge that students' work will be shared with authentic audiences outside the classroom can strongly encourage students to make this transition to reader-based prose. In the face of a real audience, rather than just an imagined one, a good teacher can more easily focus students' attention on how their writing will be received by readers.

A similar principle is at work with students' multimodal productions, and a potentially wide audience exists for these products via the World Wide Web, museums, and other outlets. We witnessed projects in almost all the schools in which students produced multimedia work for authentic audiences. Here we highlight two such projects that we found especially interesting.

Game Design at Henry Elementary

Young people are fascinated with games, but their interest in games is seldom exploited for school-based learning (Gee, 2003, 2004). A highly creative project at Henry Elementary School involved students both in designing a game and designing their own instructional video to accompany the game.

The project was organized as part of the school's commitment to service learning, which involves students carrying out and reflecting on initiatives of benefit to others (for an overview of service learning, see Kendall, 1990; for a discussion of its relevance to educational technology, see Warschauer & Cook, 1999). In this project, students in a split third- and fourth-grade class in the school's gifted program were assigned to design age-appropriate games for teaching mathematics to the school's second-grade students. In groups of four, the third and fourth graders began by logging onto the Internet to find the California state standards for second-grade math. After choosing one standard as the focus of their game, they developed math activities such as die-rolling and counting games to review the concepts and provide opportunities for practice. They then composed written directions for playing the games, a process that required multiple revisions of their written texts until their language was sufficiently simplified for their younger audience. Finally, before launching their games into the second-grade classroom, each group developed a multimedia video explaining how to play the game. As with the written texts, students carefully crafted the language of their videos to make sure that it would be understandable for second graders.

I will return to this project in the next chapter, as I think it represents a fascinating example of the use of laptops for promoting flexible and creative habits of mind. For now, though, the main point is that having to produce a game and video for a particular audience very much focused the attention of these elementary school students.

Four Freedoms at Castle Middle

In the previous chapter I introduced learning expeditions at Castle Middle, discussing their relationship to information literacy. What is relevant here is that almost every one of these expeditions results in a collaborative multimedia creation to be shared with the public. This is in line with the school's strategic focus on what has been termed *representing-to-learn* (Zemelman, Daniels, & Hyde, 1998, p. 194). Expanding on a previous concept of writing-to-learn, representing-to-learn simply means that students learn best when they are required to continually represent what they have learned through texts, art, music, drama, or other products or performance media, and that learning is further enhanced when the products are shared with the public through performances, displays, and websites.

An excellent example of this is the Four Freedoms expedition completed by eighth-grade students at the school. In this 10-week expedition, students drew on a 1941 speech by Franklin Roosevelt and a subsequent series of paintings by Norman Rockwell to examine freedom of speech, freedom of worship, freedom from fear, and freedom from want. Using magazine materials, the students produced art collages on one of these four freedoms to explore how the ideas of freedom change over time and how some people's freedoms may conflict with others. The students then wrote commentaries in which they explained the significance of their collages. Finally, the students assembled the commentaries and collages both in posters that were exhibited at the Maine College of Art and in a hypertext that was published on the World Wide Web.

In working on this project, students had to keep two audiences in mind—the museum attendees and users of the World Wide Web. The collages they produced were for the most part thought provoking, and their commentaries were helpful for guiding the reader to understand them.

Finally, both the game design and four freedom projects show the interesting relationship between digital media and physical artifacts. In the first example, students produced a hands-on game using poster board, dice, and other material, but they supplemented the physical artifact with an instructional video. In the second example, students produced physical collages out of magazine cutouts, but then created a website incorporating digitized versions of the collages and their essays. Both these examples are illustrative of how the laptop classroom, as any good classroom, incorporates a wide range of artifacts and resources, whether from the digital or material realm.

CONCLUSION

In this chapter I have highlighted many of the interesting forms of multimodal production that we witnessed in the laptop classroom. Such projects provided students important new outlets for knowledge representation and construction and also helped develop their multimedia literacy. Also important, students were highly engaged while working on these projects. One teacher we interviewed at Flower School described students as "technology sponges." While that was true, we also found them perhaps to be more accurately described as "multimedia sponges." We witnessed tremendous student enthusiasm when working with digital images, video, and music. For example, during one lesson on the American eagle, several children in the class immediately and excitedly imported the pictures of eagles they found on websites and replaced their desktop wallpaper with them. The educational significance of such an action is hard to evaluate, but it is a small indicator of how strongly imagery appeals to students.

Most important, in the strong majority of cases, we believe that engagement was put to good effect, as students became motivated to interact more seriously and intensively with academic content. For example, students in a third-grade class used Keynote or iMovie software to produce presentations on local history incorporating photos they took of local historical sites during a school field trip. The teacher felt strongly, and I agree, that the multimodal and interactive aspect of this assignment—incorporating students' own original photography—made local history more memorable for them. Similarly, we witnessed fifth- and sixth-grade students show brief videos they had made demonstrating each of the Bill of Rights. We have no doubt that these students will better remember those 10 Amendments, and why they are important, than other students who simply memorized them for a test.

Of course, these benefits are not always achieved. As with technology more generally, we sometimes witnessed shallow uses of multimedia, as seen in the student PowerPoint presentations on subcultures described in Chapter 5. Indeed, presentation software (e.g., PowerPoint, Keynote) was probably the multimedia tool most frequently used ineffectively, as is so often the case outside the classroom too. However, the overall quality of multimedia-oriented instruction in laptop schools was higher than we had previously witnessed in typical schools. We believe that this was because the constant access to multimedia resources allowed teachers and students to get beyond technical instruction (e.g., here's how you create a PowerPoint slide) to focus on more substantive academic and artistic matters.

The affordances of such constant access were well summarized by a junior high teacher in California:

A lot of teachers that aren't in a one-to-one program say, "Well, how do you do technology on top of everything else you have to do?" I think the mind-set has to be, "It's not on top of everything. It's the foundation of everything."

In today's world, imagery, video, and audio—and combinations of these with each other and with texts—are already the foundation of knowledge production outside the classroom. As seen by the projects discussed in this chapter, one-to-one laptop programs help make them the foundation of knowledge representation and literacy in the K–12 classroom as well.

CHAPTER 7

Habits of Mind

I see my daughter spending time and energy and excitement on projects that I have never seen before. I've told several people, I think she spent like 17 hours one weekend working on a presentation that she was going to be doing Monday at the harbor. Her class was going down to the oceanography institute down at the harbor and she had been made a leader of several groups of kids and it was her job to be sort of the editor and compiler of all of their materials and put it into one cohesive report, but they then would share with other kids from other schools when they got down there. And the number of times that she would bring it over to me and say, "Oh, here Dad, I am doing this, I am doing that, and this is what I am going to be doing" were phenomenal. That whole weekend she was held up and working on it trying to get it to the point where she was satisfied with it.

—School district administrator/
Parent of elementary student at Flower School

The development of academic literacy cannot be reduced to a list of competencies, whether in traditional areas (e.g., reading and writing) or new ones (information literacy and media design). Rather, underlying all these skills are "habits of mind" (Intersegmental Committee of the Academic Senates, 2002, p. 12) consisting of perceptions, behaviors, attitudes, and dispositions. Though these habits of mind are extremely important in shaping people's social futures, they are difficult to define, and even more difficult to teach. They often develop not so much from *learning about* but rather from *learning to be* (see discussion in Brown & Duguid, 2000), as students engage in what Gee (2004) refers to as a "cultural learning process." This involves apprenticeship learning from "masters" (e.g., teachers, parents, coaches, more experienced peers), with the assistance of various artifacts (texts, tools, technologies). Over time, learners take on the behavior, attitudes, and habits of mind of the masters. A medical intern learns to think and act like a doctor; a graduate student learns to think and act like a professor; a young boy, depending on the type of mentors surrounding him, might learn to think and act like a gang member, a boy scout, or any number of other identities.

In this chapter, I consider what it takes to think and act like a successful student, and how learners' experiences in one-to-one laptop programs influenced their development. I approach this from three angles—engagement, study habits, and inventive thinking—and then provide examples from two schools that had very different approaches toward developing habits of mind.

ENGAGEMENT

I briefly discussed student engagement in Chapters 2 and 6 from the perspectives of reading instruction and multimedia use. I now take a more overall look at this important concept and its relationship to laptop use, focusing on what educational psychologists have identified as the three principal types of engagement: emotional, behavioral, and cognitive (for an overview of definitions and of research on engagement, see Fredricks, Blumenfeld, & Paris, 2004). *Emotional engagement* refers to students' affective reactions in the classroom, including interest, happiness, and enthusiasm. *Behavioral engagement* entails positive conduct, such as the following of rules and adhering to classroom norms, as well as the absence of disruptive behaviors such as skipping school and getting in trouble. *Cognitive engagement* refers to students' investment in, and efforts directed toward, learning, understanding, and mastering knowledge and skills.

Before they enter school, most young children show great interest and enthusiasm for learning, and that interest propels their intellectual development (Piaget, 1970). Similarly, adults often learn and perform best when they experience what Csikszentmihalyi (1990) calls *flow*, a state of highly intense personal engagement. Yet, unfortunately, too many youth become emotionally disengaged from school, and this disengagement contributes to inattention, poor performance, and high dropout rates (Fredricks et al., 2004).

Numerous prior studies have reported increased student engagement with laptops (for an overview, see Penuel, 2005), and this was certainly confirmed by our research. A total of 73% of the students we surveyed indicated that they found school more interesting since using laptops, and 77% of teachers reported higher student interest. We witnessed these positive attitudes throughout our observations. We saw children rush to class and open their laptops to begin work before class started, or return to class during lunchtime to work further.

This enthusiasm was widespread (though not in all schools—see further discussion below) and was reflected in quantitative measures of behavioral engagement. For example, in our California schools, the largest laptop programs were at Flower School and Nancy Junior High, both in the same school district. Flower, a brand new school, experienced 98.4% attendance in its first year, the highest attendance rate in the school district and significantly higher than nonlaptop schools in the district of similar demographic profiles. Nancy, a low-SES neighborhood school that implemented the laptop program at the seventh-grade level, showed a 9% drop in seventh-grade absences from the prior year, again significantly topping districtwide attendance improvements.

Even more interesting were the disciplinary outcomes at Nancy. The school has two levels of suspension, an in-school suspension to an all-day study hall for minor infractions and an at-home suspension for more serious offenses. The number of seventh-grade students who received each of these types of suspensions annually fell sharply after the laptop program was implemented, from 90 to 76 for in-school suspensions and from 47 to 14 for the more serious at-home suspensions.

Our observations and interviews suggested why this had taken place: basically, many of the students who were previously turned off at school were now enjoying working with laptops. As one of the teachers in the school who worked principally with at-risk students explained to us,

> Last year, I had kids who were very similar— similar attitudes, similar background. They'd come in with that same look on their face, "I don't want to be here. I'm bored. I'm tired of this. I'm only here because my mom, my dad, my counselor, whoever says I have to be here." Those were the kids that I fought with all year long last year. It was like pulling teeth to get them to do anything. But the same type of kid with the same attitude, so to speak, comes in this year and you give them a laptop and you give them enough that it's interesting and their faces changed. Their demeanor has changed in some way. They get very upset when I have a substitute and they can't use the laptops because that's about the only time they don't use it.

Most interesting to us were the increased levels of cognitive engagement. Cognitive engagement entails going beyond minimally expected behaviors and demonstrating psychological investment in learning, reflected by willingness to work hard, flexibility in problem solving, positive coping in the face of failure, and self-regulated use of diverse learning strategies. We witnessed all of these in the laptop schools to a greater extent than we would otherwise expect. A total of 50% of students we surveyed indicated they worked harder with laptops, and 65% of teachers indicated that students take more initiative outside of class time. We heard a number of reports from parents of their children spending a great deal of time on assignments during periods of intense personal engagement that match parts of Csikszentmihalyi's description of flow.

Students' increased level of engagement reflected to a certain extent their sheer enjoyment of working with new digital media, as seen in the discussion on multimedia in the previous chapter. A student succinctly put forward this point of view in one of our surveys, when, in responding to a question about the best parts of the laptop program, he simply said, "Hey, it's a laptop. Doesn't get better than that."

Beyond that, the way that laptops were generally deployed by teachers help fulfill three types of individual needs that have been shown to be key to enhancing student engagement: *relatedness*, *autonomy*, and *competence* (Connell & Wellborn, 1990).

Relatedness

It is generally believed that students become more engaged when classroom contexts helped meet their needs for developing positive relations with the teacher, peers, and parents (Fredricks et al., 2004). Collaborative learning was ever present in the laptop classrooms, and students seemed to thoroughly enjoy working with their peers. There were several aspects of laptop computers that lent themselves to collaborative learning. First, a computer screen presents a much more visible means of showing, sharing, and collaboratively creating student work than does a piece of paper. Second, the broader affordances of laptops, such as their multimodality and their access to online information, encouraged teachers to organize more project work, which in turn multiplied opportunities for collaboration. Finally, computer-mediated communication, such as using computer-assisted classroom discussion, provided another means of student collaboration. With students often working together on enjoyable class projects, students could, at least sometimes, develop more relaxed and enjoyable relations with their teachers, who were able to act more as mentors than drillmasters. Finally, the project work in some cases provided excellent opportunities for students to showcase quality products for their peers, parents, and family members.

The many scenes we encountered of students enthusiastically working with each other and with their teachers, and of proudly sharing work with each other and with their families, left indelible memories on our research team. These included the ThoughtPot poetry circle at Castle Middle School, in which students excitedly gathered to hear the teacher read their anonymous poetry contributions; the closing events of learning expeditions at Castle, where students delightedly watched the CD that their peers had produced of their collaborative project; the dozens of times at River Elementary, Howard Middle, and Melville High we saw students gathered around screens and animatedly discussing what should be included in a paper or presentation; and the look we saw on students' faces as they presented their video, slide presentations, and other creative productions at parent-community events at Flower School, Nancy Junior High, and Henry Elementary.

Autonomy

People also have a need for autonomy, or a desire to do things for personal reasons rather than under the control of others, and it is assumed that fulfilling such a need among students increases their engagement (Connell & Wellborn, 1990).

A high degree of student autonomy was one of the most striking features of the one-to-one laptop programs we observed. By using computer- and Internet-based resources, teachers were able to engage students in much more independent forms of learning than in a typical classroom. Just to provide one very typical example, consider instruction on Internet safety. This is an important topic in all schools, because even if children do not have laptops they are still having some opportunities to use the Internet at school and, in many cases, at home. In a typical class, students would merely be handed an information sheet on acceptable use of the Internet and be expected to follow the guidelines. However, at Nancy Junior High, a language arts teacher involved her students in producing a video public service announcement about Internet safety (briefly mentioned in Chapter 5 as an example of a promotional or advertising production). This involved two major highly autonomous components: first, deciding what aspects of Internet safety are most important for children to be aware of, and then deciding how to put together a brief video presentation that can best communicate that message. Other levels of autonomous work were embedded within (in storyboarding, filming, editing, and so on). There were undoubtedly all sorts of valuable language lessons involved, which is why the teacher felt justified to include this in the language arts curriculum (in materials made available to the students, she identified six separate reading, writing, and speaking standards that the lesson addressed). Beyond that though, the students gained the opportunity for autonomous thinking and multimedia production, as well a positive opportunity to collaborate with their peers.

It was interesting to us to note that the way autonomous learning was carried out varied a great deal among schools and teachers. Especially at the high-SES schools, students were often given a great deal of physical autonomy, including permission to wander around the classroom or in the halls or schoolyard to work with their classmates on project work, even during class periods. At other schools, and more notably in low-SES communities, students usually faced tighter rules. For example, Ms. Patterson, featured in Chapter 1 as an outstanding teacher at Nancy Junior High, ran what could only be described as a very tight ship, requiring students to all sit quietly before being allowed to open their computers. But whether operating under relaxed or strict behavioral rules, students were nevertheless in almost all cases given more intellectual and creative autonomy in the laptop classroom.

Competence

Finally, students' opportunity to experience and demonstrate their competence is also believed, with good reason, to contribute to higher engagement (Connell & Wellborn, 1990). We found that students' work with multimedia proved especially valuable for this, as it provided additional avenues for students to develop and demonstrate their expertise. Interestingly, this proved particularly helpful for children in special education programs, who due to learning or cognitive disabilities may have experienced difficulty with standard forms of text-based learning. A national survey of more than 200 special education teachers in Maine (Harris & Smith, 2004), as well as our own interviews and observations, confirmed the important role of the laptop program in helping students with special needs experience and demonstrate competence in learning.

For example, while we were visiting Howard Middle School in Maine, a seventh-grade teacher called us over excitedly to tell us about a student of hers, Ronald, who had created a PowerPoint presentation and who wanted to share it with me. "Tears are coming to my eyes," said the teacher, "because I haven't seen work like this from this kid all year long." I later spoke at length with Ronald and his mother, who explained to me that Ronald had speech and language delays and had been diagnosed with Asperger's syndrome. She spoke with great emotion about her son, and her comments reflected those of other parents we interviewed:

This is his first experience with a laptop and this year he's blossomed so much. He learned this year his PowerPoint presentations and he got a few pointers from the IT person at school and then he came up with these presentations that were amazing. I couldn't believe it. They did a unit on the West and they had an open house for parents, and I went and I was so impressed. The kids worked so hard pulling this thing together and Ryan was the only one that had a presentation that he actually did like almost like a tutorial through his presentation on Sequoia, the Indian. I still talk about it because he did such a great job. He's really trying and I'm just so proud that he is actually putting forth the effort instead of just throwing his hands up and giving up. And where his penmanship is very poor, he feels very successful by being able to use the laptop at his leisure really, and all of his teachers understand that 95% of his work is done on the laptop. He wants to know more, he's talking about doing digital movies and doing Claymation, you know, expanding on that, and that was all part of the PowerPoint presentation. And doing text documents, he feels successful in producing work that you know everybody can read not just him, because really, his handwriting, unless he really, really sweats over it, is really hard to read. He's trying more and he's not as timid about taking his projects and lessons to the next level. He really wants to please and he wants to succeed. Whereas before he might have just been more hesitant because he didn't feel successful, now he feels that success.

Caveats

Before leaving the topic of engagement, it is necessary to put forward a few important caveats. First, the extent and nature of student engagement using laptops was highly dependent on social context, including the norms and values of the school and community, students' individual abilities and beliefs, and teacher's approaches. Though there were some students like Ronald, described above, who went through transformations, in most cases changes were far more incremental. For example, in low-SES schools, such as Nancy, where there was little prior tradition of students completing much homework, this did not change radically. A total of 39% of Nancy teachers indicated that their students took more initiative outside of class using laptops, whereas at high-SES Flower School across town, where students already were in the habit of doing a lot of homework, 93% of teachers said their students took more initiative outside of class.

And at one of the ten schools, Plum High in Maine, the broader trend was student disengagement rather than engagement. As indicated in Chapter 5, laptops there were often put to poor pedagogical use, and this was exacerbated by other problems, such as ineffective use of block scheduling and difficulties in establishing and maintaining school rules. As a result of instructional, classroom management, and school management problems, students spent a great deal of time instant-messaging, surfing the web for personal entertainment, and engaging in other nonacademic activities. In addition, a much larger than ordinary percentage of students could not use their laptops on any given day due to forgetting to charge them, leaving them at home, or having damaged them. From our observations at Plum, we concluded that while a one-to-one laptop program can make a good school better, it will not fundamentally alter a school with problems. Rather, by presenting so many additional distractions, laptops connected to the Internet can exacerbate problems that exist in a poorly organized classroom or school.

I will return to the question of variation among schools at the end of this chapter, when I look at the development of habits of mind in two laptop programs in California.

STUDY HABITS

Even if students are engaged, they may not have the requisite study skills and habits to do well in school, such as organizing their learning materials, keeping track of assignments, and taking good notes. This is particularly the case for students whose families have less social, cultural, and financial capital to support them in learning such skills.

One of the unexpected findings of our research was the extent to which laptops served as a positive tool for helping students organize their work. A number of the teachers commented on this fact, especially in schools serving low-SES students. As Mr. Molina, a teacher in an elementary school in a low-SES Latino community, told us,

> We were able to do a lot of new things and projects because computers have the ability to save, whereas, with most paper assignments, students tend to lose them or trash them or destroy them. It was very hard to keep students from going on a long term project, at least at this school. It was because they

didn't really have the organizational skills and they didn't have the structured environment at home where they could keep a folder organized and not lose papers or destroy them. But the computers allowed us to do projects that went over the course of a couple of weeks, depending on how long we were working on something.

In contrast to the less-than-stellar reports we heard about students' ability to keep track of their hard-copy material, students, teachers, and parents all spoke to us enthusiastically about students' use of computers to keep and organize their work digitally. Students took notes on computer much more frequently than they did by hand, either because they preferred to write on computer, or because they found their computer-based notes more legible, easier to edit or highlight, or less likely to get lost. Some teachers worked to foster these skills and habits with special instruction on note taking or by allowing students to use notes on their tests.

Students also created computer-made flashcards with Apple's Keynote program and used them eagerly to review terms and concepts. Students organized their schoolwork—including, for example, multiple drafts of their papers—in different folders on their computers corresponding to class and semester, and told us in interviews how much better organized this made them. They also liked being able to submit work electronically to their teachers, for example, via online drop boxes.

For many students, being able to work on one portable computer seemed to provide a greater sense of independent academic identity. As a parent of a fifth-grade student at Flower school explained to us,

> One of the best things about my daughter being involved in the laptop program was the degree of independence and ownership that she developed with her taking care of her own work. Traditionally, kids have the binders. You sit down at the kitchen table and you do homework under the supervision of mom and dad checking on it. With her laptop, she's able to personalize some of her work, program her laptop. It's hers. She knows it inside and out. She's the one that logs onto the computer. She takes care of her work on her own. It hasn't left parents out of it because she has that desire to share with us, "Look at what I've done, look at the project I'm working on." But it's her laptop. She's the one that carries it all. There's just a sense of personalization with her laptop where it's hers. The independence

that I've seen in her and her work this year is much better than I thought.

Such individual and personalized study is an often-overlooked benefit of laptop programs, and one that is not easily replicable in other technology-intensive educational environments. Even the best array of shared-use computers, such as laptop carts or desktop computers in classrooms or computer labs, will not allow students to have what one of our seventh-grade interviewees termed as her own "portable study guide."

INVENTIVE THINKING

Being an engaged learner and having good study habits will only get a student so far. To be successful in advanced academic work, as well as in the prestigious and well-paying symbolic analyst careers of the twenty-first century, requires *inventive thinking*. Inventive thinking has been posited as one of the main cornerstones of twenty-first-century skills and analyzed as including the following components (see North Central Regional Educational Laboratory & The Metiri Group, 2003):

> *Adaptability and Managing Complexity*: The ability to alter one's behavior, thinking process, or attitude to to better respond to the needs of diverse contexts and environments in both today's world and the future; and the ability to handle multiple needs of different environments; and the ability to handle multiple objectives, tasks, and inputs, while responding to constraints of time, resources, and organizational or technological systems.
> *Self-Direction*: The ability to set learning objectives, plan for the accomplishment of those objectives, autonomously manage time and effort, and independently evaluate the quality of learning and of learning products.
> *Curiosity*: The desire for knowledge that leads to inquiry.
> *Creativity*: The act of making something that is new and original, whether to an individual or to a broader culture or society.
> *Risk Taking*: The willingness to make mistakes, put forth uncommon or unpopular positions, or take on difficult problems without clear solutions, so that one's personal growth, integrity, or achievements are enhanced.

Higher-Order Thinking and Sound Reasoning: The cognitive processes of analysis, comparison, inference, interpretation, synthesis, and evaluation in a variety of domains and problem-solving contexts.

Computers and the Internet are of course not required for teaching inventive thinking in schools, and it is certainly the case that use of new technologies will not guarantee that creative thinking is taught. In our own study, it would be far too simplistic to say that students' use of laptops in schools "caused" them to become more entrepreneurial or innovative. Rather, the ways that laptops were pedagogically deployed in most of the schools we observed were consistent with fostering entrepreneurship and innovation. Students gained more control over their study tools and environments than they had in typical classroom environments. They also gained more control over the topics they chose to pursue and the way they chose to investigate them. And, through constant immersion in digital media, they became more flexible in their use of such media, selecting among a variety of media to use depending on how they chose to communicate a message. Students assembled and reassembled their own work in school portfolios much more often then we observed in typical classrooms. Sometimes these portfolios were in print; more often they were digital. And they engaged in creative project-based work that allowed them to apply their own knowledge and skills toward tackling real-world issues and creating multimedia for authentic audiences.

These results were achieved partly due to the affordances of laptops, but also due to the beliefs and approaches of those educators who led and taught in the laptop programs we observed. Simply put, the early adopters of one-to-one laptop programs are often those educators who put a premium on creativity and innovation in the classroom. This was certainly the case with the people behind Maine's laptop program, as well as those behind several of the programs in California in our study. For example, Dr. Meese, Superintendent of Farrington School District in California, explained his own thinking behind starting a laptop project:

Previously, I think we have really tried to dissect at that pool of knowledge that's out there. We try to subdivide it into components. But, I think if teachers put their creativity into thinking, "What's a project that we can work on that is out here and how can I guide kids, how can I coach them so that they then want to know how to do certain things so they can achieve the project that we are all working on?" And I have used the example of a band. When I was a principal, the school band spent 2 months on one song. It was so deadening and unfortunately the band room was only 50 feet from my office and after about 2 weeks I had had it. I did not want to hear that song ever again. So I went to the band teacher and I said, "You know, there's a group of your kids who decided to form a band in the garage near where I live and I mean I've watched those kids progress from noise to some pretty good stuff in about 2 months." I said, "You know if you have a project that these kids are going towards, they could learn this stuff a lot quicker." I said, "By the way, Christmas time I want you to have a concert, put on some things," and the guy just turned white on me. And I said, "You guys can do it, I know you can." Well he almost quit on me but he went home and thought it over. Long story short, came Christmas time we had one heck of a concert. That year on they had multiple performances and the whole level was tremendously higher because they had an expectation they were going to be there and they had a project in mind. They had an ultimate goal they were trying to get to as opposed to we are going to teach you all the notes that happened to be in this series.

Meese explained to me that his vision in launching the laptop program was to give students more of the same kinds of experiences as that school band had—learning through creative expression, rather than through memorization. Our observations and interviews suggested that this was largely achieved, not only at the three schools in his district but throughout the study. However, as with other aspects of laptop use, there was variation across schools in promoting habits of mind, due both to social context and to teacher beliefs.

To examine this variation, we look at two markedly different one-to-one laptop programs in California. The first, at Henry Elementary School, was located in the school's Gifted and Talented Education (GATE) Program, and was designed to further the goals of that program. The second, at Freedom Middle School, was situated in an alternative education program, and was designed to help meet that program's goals.

INVENTIVE THINKING IN A GIFTED PROGRAM

Henry Elementary School is located in a middle-class suburban neighborhood of Southern California. The school's GATE program, which serves both the local neighborhood and surrounding school neighborhoods, consists of two classes, a third/fourth-grade class and a fifth/

sixth-grade class. About half the students in the program are White, nearly half are Asian or Asian American, and a few are Latino. The two teachers in the program are highly talented instructors with a great deal of positive experience in integrating technology into instruction prior to the one-to-one laptop program. The laptop program was launched within the GATE program in 2004–05; parents in the program agreed to lease laptops for their children, with low-income parents eligible for financial assistance from the school.

As with other GATE programs, the focus of instruction in the two classes was geared to developing advanced thinking skills. In Mr. Spratt's third/fourth-grade class, a large wall poster highlights 11 aspects for "depth and complexity" in learning, urging the 8- and 9-year-old students to focus on *Unanswered questions, Language of the disciplines, Different perspectives, Big idea, Across disciplines, Ethics, Details, Rules, Relate across time, Trends,* and *Patterns.* Another poster lists nine key "scholarly attributes": *Show academic humility, Show curiosity, Be prepared with learning tools, Consider multiple points of view, Save ideas, Take time to ponder, Exercise the intellect, Recognize the knowledge available,* and *Set goals.*

Mr. Spratt refers to both of these posters as he explains the goals of his class to me. Promoting deeper, more complex learning and developing scholarly attributes are key to his instructional goals, and he has found laptops an invaluable tool for achieving those goals. Students in his course engage in numerous highly creative projects, several of which have been mentioned or described in this book, such as a holiday shopping project (Chapter 5), a video promotion inviting tourists to a planet (Chapter 6), and a game design project (Chapter 6). This latter project is particularly interesting for showing the habits of mind that Spratt attempts to promote in his young learners, and the multiple levels of analytic thinking required. In designing the game, students first had to interpret the relationship between second graders' current interest and skills and mathematics standards laid out for them by the state of California. Next they had to design an educational intervention that would be interesting to children, effective in helping them reach the standards, and possible to materially develop into a game. Then, they had to design, film, and edit their video, which included both spoken instructions and physical demonstrations, at a level appropriate for younger children. The project required—and the students demonstrated—a level of sophistication not often expected of 8- and 9-year-old students in U.S. schools.

The pedagogy underlying this project looks very different from that of a traditional classroom. First, the students conducted independent research on the Internet and located the appropriate state level standards for second-grade math. In a typical classroom, the teacher would most likely have taken this step beforehand and then assigned groups of students to preselected math concepts. Second, the students collaborated in groups of four to discuss what types of activities would engage their target second-grade audience and negotiated a collaborative, multiday project plan to guide their decisions and regulate their time. Such autonomy in project-based learning is rare in conventional classrooms, in which teachers often require that students follow a predetermined sequence of steps. Third, students used both linguistic means (a direction booklet) as well as multimodal means (digital explanatory videos) to create age-appropriate instructional materials, a step that would often be completely overlooked in other peer-teaching scenarios, in which older students are typically given prefabricated scripts to follow as they work with younger peers. Finally, throughout the process, these young children dealt with cognitively complex tasks of breaking down knowledge and repackaging it, of transforming information from one mode to another, and of redesigning the pedagogy of math drills that typically inform test preparation in schools. Such multimodal pedagogies help to position students not as recipients of knowledge, but rather, as Luke (2003) suggests, as students actively drawing on blends of new and old learning styles and practices.

Beyond their work on particular class projects, Spratt's students are also heavily involved in managing the day-to-day operations of the classroom. The class is organized like a city, complete with a city council and administrative leadership made up of a judge, interior manager, police officer, health officer, technology team, and city treasurer. Making ample use of technology (to make posters, keep minutes, carry out communications, and so on), the elected officers fulfill a variety of roles. For example, the student judge organizes the weekly caseload and runs the court, facilitates "city" discussions of rules and policies, chooses weekly student spotlight award winners for exemplary behavior, judges student irresponsible behavior violations during field trips and substitute teacher days, and works with the city police, inspectors, and treasurer to enforce all rules.

In summary, Mr. Spratt's teaching moves beyond the traditional curriculum to develop his GATE students' abilities to develop deep and complex understanding and take broad entrepreneurial leadership for their learning and their lives. These were his goals prior to using laptops as well, when he also taught in the GATE program. However, he has found laptops a very helpful tool for achieving his goals:

A great benefit of the laptop program is being able to integrate across the curriculum, go deeper. Students can complete projects faster and in a more authentic fashion. They can organize the whole class themselves. I attribute that to having the tool to work with. The students are constructing their own learning.

SELF-REGULATION IN AN ALTERNATIVE EDUCATION PROJECT

The laptop program we observed at Freedom Middle School represents a radically different context for implementation of technology. Freedom School is located in a low-income inner-city neighborhood a half hour away from the suburbs of Henry Elementary. An Alternative Education program has been established at the school for eighth-grade students who are on the verge of being expelled from school due to consistent truancy, disruptive or unacceptable behavior, or being on probation with the juvenile court system (see discussion in Johnson, 2003). The alternative program is designed to help students get back on track so they can continue their education. Students spend the entire school day in a self-contained classroom taught by Ms. Velasquez with the assistance of a full-time aide, Mr. Paul.

Ms. Velasquez defines her main goals for the course in attitudinal and behavioral terms rather than in reference to academic standards. She explained her main objective for her students:

To empower them. To realize that it's all in their grasp. It's all within them to do better. It doesn't matter if they have a bad teacher or a good teacher. It's their will that will make them do better. Doesn't matter where you are or where you're from. It's within you to do better. You can't let a teacher or a student or somebody else disempower you and have you get bad grades because of them. It's you and that's my main objective is to let them realize that they're the ones in control of their lives and how they do in school, not somebody else.

The laptops for the course were provided through a grant from Apple computer, together with a number of digital cameras and multimedia software. Ms. Velasquez deploys the equipment in service of her overall goals.

One of her favorite activities that she has done each year with the laptops is an end-of-term multimedia project. In the project, students put together a photo essay reflecting on their lives, and in particular on their behavior and attitudes in relationship to school. Using graphic organizing software, they plot out a story composed of three parts: where they were before they entered the alternative education program (in terms of attitude, behavior, and so on), how they have changed in the program, and where they are now as they look ahead to the future. Then using the digital cameras and scanners, they work with prior and new photos plus captions to produce their essays, which are printed out in nice books for the students to take home with them. Though the photo essays were produced after we had completed observations at the school, Ms. Velasquez emphasized to us how helpful a similar project the prior year had been for enhancing student pride.

Ms. Velasquez also used the laptops in a more direct disciplinary fashion. Students who disrupted class were in danger of having their laptops taken away from them temporarily, in which case they were required to sit in the back of the room and use an older desktop computer.

The largest laptop-based project that took place during the year involved a lengthy interdisciplinary unit on eighteenth-century American history. In order to make the U.S. revolution more relevant to her students' lives, Ms. Velasquez had her students complete a number of writing projects comparable to those of the American revolutionaries and founders, including pamphlets (protesting conditions in the classroom), a petition (requesting changes in the school), and a mock constitution (encompassing desired school rules). Laptops were used for research, writing, editing, and formatting.

The implementation of this project provided a fascinating glimpse of how Ms. Velasquez used the curriculum and technology to achieve greater self-regulation among her students. For example, on one of her observation days, students were repeatedly sent over to a microwave oven over in a corner of the room if they misbehaved in any way. While at the microwave, they were required to write out by hand a full page reflecting on their misbehavior before they could return to their seats and laptops. Ms. Velasquez and Mr. Paul started sending students over to the microwave for increasingly petty offenses, such as speaking quietly out of turn. They later revealed to me that this was part of a plan to spark emotion in the students and get them to write protest pamphlets (á la Thomas Paine's *Common Sense*). Though in this case, the object of protest was to be the microwave oven, and what it represented.

Not surprisingly, most of the students focused on the injustice that the microwave represented, as people were sent there for increasingly petty and arbitrary reasons. Some students ventured into science fiction and gave the microwave an evil will of its own. I thought all these responses were quite interesting and made great copy for a protest pamphlet. To my surprise though, Ms. Velasquez dismissed this writing as off-target, and instead greatly praised one student who wrote about how the microwave symbolized students' own misbehavior. Ms. Velasquez then explained to both me and the class that the entire purpose of the exercise was to get students to focus on how their own misbehavior led to problems, and thus to write a protest pamphlet against themselves!

What's most interesting about this lesson is the teacher's overall approach, rather than the use of technology per se. But that gets to one of the broader lessons of this chapter, and this book. Laptops have powerful affordances that allow teachers and students to better accomplish their goals in diverse circumstances. Just as students at Henry Elementary could better design a game and accompanying instructional video using laptops and the Internet, students at Freedom could better write and design a protest pamphlet. But the types of goals that are served do not necessarily change due to incorporation of laptops. While the teachers at Henry Elementary sought to develop critical thinkers in a gifted program and used laptops to that end, Ms. Velasquez sought to emphasize self-regulation in an alternative education program at Freedom Middle, and she used laptops toward her end.

CONCLUSION

In the strong majority of classrooms we observed, students became more engaged in the learning process through the use of laptops. In most schools, they also appeared to develop better study skills and habits. In addition, teachers who sought to promote critical thinking, entrepreneurship, and innovation among their students found laptops a highly flexible and effective tool for achieving these ends (and teachers who had other objectives often found laptops an effective tool for achieving those as well).

The contrasting examples between the gifted and alternative education programs, as well as the problems at Plum High mentioned earlier, make clear there is no automatic relationship between laptop use and critical thinking or any other particular habit of mind. In considering this, it is useful to keep in mind the basic triangular relationship of human activity suggested by Vygotsky of *subject, object,* and *mediational means* (see discussion in Wertsch, 1991; for a more complex model of activity theory, see Engestrom, 1987). The first element of the Vygotskian model, the subject, includes the students, classmates, and teacher. The second element is the object of study, including the topic, task, and goal. The third element of mediational means includes laptops, the Internet, software, books, handouts, or any other artifacts or tools. Each of these three elements is crucial to educational outcome, and they function together in one combined unit rather than as separable elements. The students that any school or district has a given, but schools have substantial control over objects of study and mediational means. Our investigation into 10 one-to-one laptop schools suggests that combining the appropriate content, goals, objectives, and tasks with advanced communication and information tools, as represented by wireless laptops, creates the best possibility for promoting the habits of mind required for twenty-first-century success.

CHAPTER 8

Teaching the Word
and the World

In the beginning of this book, I noted three main literacy challenges facing U.S. schools, labeled past and future, home and school, rich and poor. I also noted that, in spite of technology's promise for addressing these challenges, most previous attempts at integrating computers into schools had bogged down in problems related to limited student access. We now can weigh the data from these 10 schools in California and Maine in evaluating whether laptop programs offer a useful approach for addressing these literacy challenges.

PAST AND FUTURE

Combining what was learned from both the area of "traditional literacies" (reading and writing) and "new literacies" (information literacy and multimedia production), the changes in literacy practice in the laptop classroom can be summarized as occurring in three areas: processes, sources, and products of literacy.

Processes

Literacy practices in the laptop classroom became more autonomous, with students having greater control over content and pacing. They became more public, with greater opportunities for students and teacher to see student work. They were more frequently authentic in purpose and audience, as opposed to being only for a grade from the teacher. They were more frequently collaborative, based on student cooperation, and with a more iterative process, based on greater attention to planning and revising work. More scaffolding was provided, for example, through computer-based dictionaries, thesauruses, and spell checkers, and more feedback was provided by peers, teachers, and automated engines. As a result of all this, students more frequently found literacy activities engaging in the laptop classroom.

Sources

Students in laptop classrooms made use of a greater variety of published sources, taking advantage of the huge amount of material available online, either on the public Web or through proprietary information services, such as EBSCO. Students also made greater use of empirical data, either gathered from the Web or collected in the classroom (e.g., using computer-connected scientific probes). Finally, students were better able to archive their own prior work and experiences (e.g., via digital video) as a source for analysis and reflection.

Products

Students in laptop classrooms produced a wider variety of textual genres, including brochures, newspapers, petitions, posters, and business letters. They also produced considerable more multimedia of diverse genres, including not only slide presentations (not uncommon in typical classrooms), but also musical compositions, videos, animation, and websites.

These benefits were recognized by students, teachers, and administrators, all of whom spoke to us in interviews about the importance of technology use for students' futures, as well as the importance of other related curricular changes, such as greater emphasis on planning and completing projects.

The rationale of career preparation for educational technology has often been criticized, since schools need to be about more than job training (e.g., see discussion in Postman, 1995). In addition, a narrow focus on "computer literacy" is seen as a waste of time, either because students develop such skills out of school or because computer programs change rapidly, and the programs they learn today might not be needed in the future (see discussion in Oppenheimer, 2004). What's more, whatever computer skills students will actually need in future occupations can be learned fairly quickly on the job.

However, while these criticisms might be valid for many educational uses of technology, which often tend to overly focus on technical training (e.g., see Warschauer, Knobel, & Stone, 2004), our investigation suggests they are not applicable to most one-to-one laptop programs. Instead, the constant access to computers and the Internet in these programs allows teachers to move beyond teaching technology as a separate skill, and instead focus on broad and purposeful learning activities that incorporate technology. This shift toward broader and more purposeful learning activities, as seen in the changes in literacy processes, sources, and outcomes described above, represent not vocational training but rather preparation of students with the kinds of thinking, analysis, and communication skills needed for a wide range of important careers and for other forms of societal participation in the twenty-first century.

In summary, preparing students better for the future is probably the single greatest benefit of laptop programs, as demonstrated on a regular basis in this study.

HOME AND SCHOOL

The laptop programs we observed were also highly successful in overcoming unproductive contradictions between home and school for students. First, students were able to experience in the classroom many of the media-rich activities that they carry out at home, such as working with digital audio, imagery, and video. Of course the purpose of school is not to duplicate the home environment; students spend many hours a week passively watching television at home, and few people suggest that that should be duplicated at school. The difference is that, in contrast to watching TV, analyzing and producing multimedia is critically important for knowledge production in today's world, so such multimedia activities can and should be integrated into the school curriculum. In other words, laptops allow pedagogical and curricular approaches that are both substantively important and highly engaging. What's more, when students work with multimedia at school, they are doing so in a different way than they usually do at home. Whatever students learn from playing videogames or using multimedia for other uses at home (a considerable amount, according to some scholars; see Gee, 2003), it seldom directly focuses on the academic content of science, social studies, and language arts that school-based instruction involved. In addition, while a few students teach themselves sophisticated multimedia production, most students have neither the home resources nor support to master such production at home and must instead rely on school-based instruction for learning how to compose and produce in diverse multimedia genres. Laptop programs were thus able to capture students' enthusiasm for using new technologies and, at least in most cases, use that to focus on the mastery of academic content and the development of academic literacies.

Laptop programs also helped overcome the home-school disconnect in a more direct way—by providing a learning tool that could be brought home. Eight of the ten one-to-one programs we investigated permitted students to bring laptops home. Students and their parents frequently spoke to us about the benefits that this brought about for their learning. For students who didn't have another computer at home, the laptop provided an especially valuable resource, as they could work on school activity (such as writing or editing papers), even if they didn't have home Internet access. In many cases, students did have access to another computer in the home environment, but that computer was less than ideal for use in studying or homework, either because it was outdated, lacked appropriate software, or was shared with family members and thus not regularly available. Especially interesting to us was what we heard from students who did have regular access to another modern computer at home. In such cases, students usually preferred having one dedicated portable laptop where they could do and keep all their homework, rather than dividing schoolwork between two computers. They thus completed more computer-related homework via their laptop than they had completed in the past on their home computer (supporting related findings by Russell et al., 2004; see discussion in Chapter 1 above). For many students, being able to work on one portable computer seemed to provide a greater sense of home-school continuity.

This increased ability to coordinate home and school activity was easy for me to understand when I thought about my own struggles to integrate home and office computing, for example, through use of flash drives, portable hard drives, or servers, prior to use of a laptop. Not surprisingly, I and a lot of other information workers find such home-office integration to be much smoother when bringing a laptop back and forth; it is hardly a surprise that students also find use of a laptop helps overcome their home-school divide. Of course the broader significance of this easing of the home-office divide for workers is mixed, with the benefits of being able to work from home matched up against the disadvantages of sometimes feeling compelled to work from home. For students, however, they, their parents, and their teachers all described greater use of laptops at home for learning as very positive, with the main negative factor being the physical burden in carrying the laptop back and forth from school. (In the future, this problem will likely be offset by the decreasing weight of laptops as well as the likely reduction in numbers and size of textbooks, as material shifts to electronic environments.) Of course, students did many other things with their laptops at home besides studying, such as playing games, but the parents we interviewed did not point to these additional uses as problematic.

Two of the schools we observed did not allow students to take their computers home, due to possible problems with loss or breakage and lack of district, school, or parent money for insurance. Unfortunately, both of these schools were in low-SES neighborhoods. Thus, at least from this small sample size of 10 schools, it appears that, in some cases, those students who might be least likely to have computer access at home were less likely to be able to bring their laptop home. (This relates to the third literacy challenge, between rich and poor, discussed next.)

RICH AND POOR

The gap between rich and poor proved far more challenging to overcome than the gaps between past and future and between home and school. This is not surprising, given how pervasive, substantial, and mutually reinforcing economic and educational inequities are in the United States (Day & Newburger, 2002; Kozol, 2005).

There were some special benefits of the laptop program for low-SES students. First, fewer low-income students had regular access to a computer at home and thus had potentially more to gain by being in a laptop program. Indeed, the low-income parents we interviewed were especially enthusiastic about the laptop programs (and usually more so than their high-income counterparts) because they saw the programs as providing opportunities not otherwise available to their children. For example, at Plum High in Maine, in a rural and low-income neighborhood, several of the parents felt that the school's laptop program—albeit flawed in our eyes (see discussion in Chapter 7)—had contributed to important new study and career possibilities for their children.

We also took note of the benefits of increased student engagement in low-SES schools, many of whose students are especially turned off to formal education. These benefits were exemplified by the sharp reduction in suspensions at Nancy Junior High in California (see discussion in Chapter 7).

At the same time, we also noted countervailing tendencies. Simply put, low-SES students and the schools that served them were often less prepared than higher SES students and schools to take advantage of the full capability of laptops. Students in these schools tended to have fewer language and literacy skills, and this limited what they could accomplish with laptops. For students with low reading or writing skills, even searching for a simple term on the Internet was a challenge. Similarly, working independently with automated essay feedback was difficult for students who could not comprehend the meaning of the feedback or understand the grammatical terms used. In addition, low-SES students had had less access to computers at home in their lives, which meant they had fewer keyboarding skills, less knowledge of computer programs, and a lesser likelihood of having computer-savvy parents or siblings The learning curve was thus greater for their use of laptop computers. This of course was multiplied in the two low-SES schools in which students were not permitted to take the laptops home. And finally, there were other elements related to the culture of learning in low-SES schools—including disciplinary problems at some schools and weak traditions of assigning and doing homework at other schools—that mitigated against leveraging laptops for school and student improvement.

In contrast, the implementation of laptop programs in high-SES schools tended to go smoother. Teachers, facing fewer serious discipline problems and with far fewer at-risk learners (e.g., English-language learners, students lacking basic reading skills), had an easier time in planning content-rich lessons taking advantage of online material or involving autonomous learning. Students had a lot of collective computer experience and keyboarding skills, as well as the support of more technologically skilled parents. A larger number of parents volunteered in the classroom, which provided another resource for assisting technology-enhanced project work.

For all these reasons, the implementation of laptop programs at the low-SES schools was more challenging, and the outcomes more mixed. Some low-SES schools did an excellent job of integrating laptops into instruction while others were clearly struggling. In contrast, each of the high-SES schools we observed had a very successful laptop program.

These differences between low- and high-SES schools run against one of the common rationales of laptop programs, repeated to us many times by teachers and administrators in this study: Laptop programs help overcome educational inequity. Yet such differences are consistent with what has occurred following other reforms involving technology or media, which though targeted at low-income populations are often best exploited by the more privileged sectors that can leverage their preexisting educational, social, and cultural resources. This outcome became famous in connection with the Sesame Street educational television show (Cook et al., 1975), and since has come to be known as the "Sesame Street effect" (Attewell & Battle, 1999, p. 1).

Due to the small size of our study, the lack of random sampling, and the difficulty of weighing competing outcomes (e.g., the benefits low-SES students gained from obtaining new access to computers versus the benefits that high-SES students gained from more rapidly exploiting technology-mediated learning opportunities), I cannot conclusively say that the laptop programs in this study widened educational divides, nor can I say they helped narrow them. Further investigation, for example, by quantitatively comparing changes in test-score results across low- and high-SES schools throughout the state of Maine, would shed more light on this issue. Even that, though, would prove far from definitive, not only due to the insensitivity of test scores to measuring the benefits of laptop programs, but also due to the relative newness of laptop programs there and elsewhere in the United States. For example, the comparative advantages that high-SES students have in first using laptops may fade over time as their low-SES counterparts gain the experience and skills to also benefit fully from one-to-one programs.

All of this begs the question of whether laptop programs are distributed equally across U.S. schools to begin with. Since there is no national listing of one-to-one laptop programs, this question is impossible to answer. However, it is—though troubling—worth noting that two of the laptop programs discussed in this study, both launched by grants and both in low-SES schools, have ended since the study was completed. In one case, at Freedom Middle School in California, a number of the laptops were stolen or damaged; and lacking replacement funds, the one-to-one program ended. At River Elementary School, also in California, which had such a promising pilot laptop program (see discussion in Chapter 3), the principal was transferred to Gleason Ridge Elementary School in a high-SES neighborhood across town. He later recruited both River's assistant principal, Mr. Truman, and laptop teacher, Mr. Molina, to join him at Gleason Ridge, and River's educational technology coordinator left to take a district position. With all the personnel who launched and taught in the laptop program at River gone, the school's one-to-one program collapsed and the laptops went unused for a year for lack of interest from River's teachers. The following year, the district redistributed the laptops to Gleason Ridge, where they are now being used by the same teacher as before, Mr. Molina, but with very different students (including part of the school's Gifted and Talented Education program, but without any English-language learners).

This is an excellent example of the broader social context—with experienced administrators and teachers often transferring to high-SES schools and pulling other resources along with them—that shapes schooling in the United States, including the implementation of educational technology programs. Educational technology programs, even those as powerful as one-to-one computing, will never overcome the broader social and economic divisions that lead to educational inequity in the United States; that will require a much larger and more ambitious set of reforms about how schools are funded and organized.

At the same time, we have witnessed great success in low-SES schools in use of laptop programs, such as at Castle Middle School in Maine, which includes a large number of low-income students and English-language learners, yet maintains high academic standards and continually surpasses state average in test scores. Unlike other low-SES schools across the country (see Becker, 2000b; Wenglinsky, 1998), Castle does not deploy laptops to drill material into students. Rather, it engages them in meaningful inquiry toward purposeful ends, resulting in the production of high-quality products, while providing substantial scaffolding and support to students with limited language or literacy ability so that they can successfully complete their tasks. Similar approaches were taken by the most successful teachers of at-risk learners in other schools we observed.

THE FUTURE OF LAPTOP PROGRAMS

For now, one-to-one laptop programs are still relatively few in number due to their considerable costs. Even successful programs, like that in Maine or in the Farrington School District in California, are struggling to ensure their continuance. At least for the next few years, one-to-one programs will likely continue to expand slowly among "early adopters" (Rogers, 1995)—schools, districts, and state departments of education that see themselves as bold leaders in educational technology.

Yet any research on technology in education, or indeed, in society, has to consider that it is dealing with a moving target. To do otherwise would be to repeat the mistake of IBM Chairman Thomas Watson, who declared in 1943, based on current technologies, that he thought there was a world market for about five computers.

Though some critics question the very idea of computers in schools (e.g., see Healy, 1998), they are in a minority. The majority of policy makers and educators with questions about the worth of educational computing are carrying out a cost-benefit analysis, with advantages that computers bring carefully weighed against their expense, especially in the face of other possible educational reforms that are competing for the same funds. It is for this reason that, as computer prices have dropped, the numbers of computers have steadily risen in schools

(Parsad, Jones, & Greene, 2005). And within the mix of computers in school, as in the home and office, laptops are steadily gaining ground (Market Data Retrieval, 2005).

The average price of low-end laptops has fallen precipitously in recent years (from an average of $1600 in 2002 to less than $650 in 2006) and is expected to reach about $400 by 2008, reaching an equivalent level of the expected desktop price of that year (Computer Economics, 2005). Educational models have sometimes been more expensive, due in part to the strong market share of the more costly Apple line, but Apple's adoption of the Intel chip will allow it to produce lower-cost laptops too. Meanwhile, a well-publicized initiative from MIT Media Lab (2005), led by Nicholas Negroponte and with the involvement of Alan Kay and Seymour Papert, is developing a $100 laptop to be piloted in China, India, Brazil, Argentina, Egypt, Nigeria, and Thailand. Though the $100 laptop's features make it unsuitable for the U.S. market, the initiative will nevertheless put downward pressure on the broader educational laptop market.

At the same time, costs of other peripherals, such as printers and projects, will also fall, as will the costs of warranties for both computers and peripherals. Some of the cost savings attributed to laptop use will increase, as more material currently in textbooks is ported to online realms and increased penetration of laptops allows for a freeing-up of computer laboratory space.

At some point, with costs falling, a financial tipping point will be reached, and one-to-one programs will spread from a relatively small number of early adopters to the majority of schools in the United States. Eventually, one-to-one computing will be commonplace in U.S. schools, just as it is commonplace in U.S. offices. The technology involved by then will likely have considerably evolved, and may even look very different from today's laptops, but will undoubtedly share many of the essential capabilities, such as mechanisms for inputting and editing texts and other media, finding and sharing information online, and creating and publishing multimodal products.

For much of the last century, educators have been seeking to reform schools through inputs of technology and have largely failed. Earlier technologies, such as radio, film, and television, remained marginal to the educational process, in spite of the exaggerated promises of their promoters (Cuban, 1986). Computers will not suffer the same fate; anybody who thinks computers of some form will not become ubiquitous in schools, both in their presence and use, is misreading social, economic, technological, and educational trends.

At the same time ubiquity does not imply reform. And the U.S. record of integrating technology into education to date is not encouraging, especially among our neediest learners, who too often suffer from tedious drills, ineffective tutorials, or low-level project work that involves little more than cutting and pasting (Becker, 2000b; Warschauer, 2000a; Warschauer, Knobel, & Stone, 2004; Wenglinsky, 1998).

To achieve meaningful educational reform with technology, schools need to consider the real literacy and learning challenges facing our country: to prepare our students for a life in which twenty-first-century skills of digital literacy, inventive thinking, effective communication, and high productivity are more important than memorization of dates, names and facts; and to bridge the vast disconnects between home and school and rich and poor that contribute to disengagement, high dropout rates, and failure to achieve even basic literacy for large numbers of learners.

Laptops are not a magic bullet to solve our educational challenges. Multiple examples from throughout this book disprove such simple determinism. However, it is useful here to distinguish between what Levinson (1997) calls "hard and soft media determinism." The former suggests that the presence and use of certain media automatically bring determined results. The latter means that media can enable change, but do not in and of themselves bring it about. Computers and the Internet certainly enable forms of information access, communication, and knowledge production that were not possible previously, and one-to-one access to such technologies amplifies such affordances. One-to-one programs thus represent the best opportunity yet to transform education through incorporation of technology.

TEACHING THE WORD AND THE WORLD

To conclude, I want to turn to an important historical concept, that of the relationship between the *word* and the *world*. Theologians have long used the concepts of word and world to refer to the relationship between Biblical texts and society. Later, Freire and Macedo (1987) appropriated the terms to emphasize that literacy (reading and writing the word) needed to be preceded by and contribute to efforts to understand and transform society (reading and writing the world).

Though I use the terms here in neither a Biblical nor strict Freirian sense, I do think the metaphors of word and world are helpful for summarizing the affordances of laptop computers for literacy development.

On the one hand, laptops are a powerful tool for helping learners understand and manipulate text, that is, to grasp the word. Images and video can scaffold texts and provide clues for developing readers. Annotations can offer further scaffolding and encourage appropriate reading strategies. Use of different fonts, colors, and highlighting can draw attention to particular words and phrases and the relationship between them. Graphic organizing software can help students analyze texts or plan their own writing. Word processing software allows students to achieve a more iterative writing process and to carry out the formatting required for a wide variety of genres. Dictionaries, thesauruses, spelling and grammar checkers, and bibliographic software provide additional forms of support for students to improve the quality of their writing. The readability of computer-generated texts then makes them more suitable for evaluation and feedback from peer, teacher, and machine. Computer-mediated classroom discussion provides students a way to communicate in written form, thus providing further opportunities for learners to notice others' written language and hone their own writing. While these tools are potentially valuable to all students, they can have special benefit for those facing special literacy challenges, such as English-language learners, at-risk students, and learners in special education programs, inasmuch as these groups of learners may have the most need for the kinds of scaffolding and support available via computer.

On the other hand, laptop computers are a potent tool for bringing the wider world into the classroom and thus both motivating and contextualizing literacy practices. Students can discover authentic reading material on almost any topic, and be introduced to up-to-date information and perspectives from peoples and cultures across the globe. They can gather the information and resources to address diverse social issues, from how to maintain diverse ecologies to weighing the benefits and disadvantages of technological progress, to understanding why and how societies go to war. Students can then develop and publish high-quality products that can be shared with interlocutors or the public, whether in their community or internationally. And through these products, from reviews published for Amazon.com to Spanish-language books created for children in need, students can not only learn about the world, but they can also leave their mark on it.

Unfortunately, these perspectives of word and world are often separated from each other. Educational leaders and policy makers who are concerned, as they should be, about raising at-risk learners' test scores, too often grab onto narrow means to achieve these ends. The resulting scripted literacy programs or drill and practice computer activities attempt to focus students' attention on the word without bringing to bear the wider resources of the world that make the word meaningful. Not surprisingly, students view such teaching as disconnected from their lives and their community, and they disengage from school.

At the same time, many technology enthusiasts focus exclusively on the broader world and dismiss the word. In their excitement about the potential of media production, international communication, and video games for promoting student learning, they sometimes forget that stimulating environments in and of themselves do not magically transform learners. Rather, sufficient amounts of scaffolding and support are required to help learners make sense of and learn from such environments. And, crucially, the amount of scaffolding and support necessary is inversely proportional to learners' prior expertise (Kalyuga, Ayres, Chandler, & Sweller, 2003). At-risk students, including English-language learners, students with learning disabilities, and students reading behind grade level, are least able to cope with unstructured environments because such environments place too heavy a cognitive load on the learner (see discussion in Feldon, 2004). As far as literacy development goes, exposing learners to the world without providing adequate support for them to master the word is a likely way to worsen educational inequity.

The good news is that there is no reason why these two have to be separated. As seen in many of the laptop classrooms in this study, the vast amount of tools available via computer and the Internet provide an ideal environment for better teaching both the word and the world.

Recall now the conflicting views of the principal and the professor discussed at the beginning of this book. The principal was highly focused on the word, and specifically on improving his elementary school students' decoding and comprehension skills. The professor, on the other hand, was directing students' efforts to the world—to interact with the broader community, learn about local and national events, and publish a widely accessible newspaper. I speculated that these two perspectives were compatible, and in laptop classrooms across the country we have seen that to be the case. The majority of teachers we observed were creatively making use of one-to-one computing to both scaffold students' language and stretch their perspectives.

Our students today need to grasp both the word and the world. They need to comprehend and create texts, and they need to use texts and other semiotic resources as tools for interpreting and transforming society. As seen throughout this book, one-to-one computing amplifies the ability of schools to help students achieve these ends. In the coming years, more schools and districts will undoubtedly turn to one-to-one initiatives. If, in doing so, they fully exploit the affordances of wireless laptops for teaching the word, the world, and the relationship between them, then we will have taken an important step toward meeting the learning and literacy challenges our nation faces in the twenty-first century.

References

Alliance for Childhood. (2000). *Fool's gold: A critical look at computers in childhood.* College Park, MD: Author.

American Association of School Librarians & Association for Educational Communications Technology. (1998). *Information power: Building partnerships for learning.* Atlanta: American Library Association.

American Library Association. (2000). *Information literacy competency standards for higher education.* Retrieved February 2, 2006, from http://www.ala.org/ala/acrl/acrlstandards/standards.pdf

Anderson, R. E., & Ronnkvist, A. (1999). *The presence of computers in American schools: Teaching, Learning, and Computing: 1998 Survey Report.* Irvine, CA: Center for Research on Information Technology and Organizations.

Apple Computer. (2005). *Movie trailers.* Retrieved February 2, 2006, from http://www.apple.com/trailers/

Apple Computer. (2006). *Apple education.* Retrieved February 2, 2006, from http://www.apple.com/education/

Attewell, P., & Battle, J. (1999). Home computers and school performance. *The Information Society: An International Journal, 15*(1), 1–10.

Auerbach, E. (1997). The power of voice and the voices of power. In T. Menacker (Ed.), *Literacy for change: Community-based approaches: Conference proceedings* (pp. 1–15). Honolulu: University of Hawai'i, Center for Second Language Research.

Ausubel, D. (1960). The use of advance organizers in the learning and retention of meaningful verbal material. *Journal of Educational Psychology, 51,* 267–272.

Badger, R., & White, G. (2000). A process genre approach to teaching writing. *ELT Journal, 54*(2), 153–160.

Baynham, M. (1993). Code switching and mode switching: Community interpreters and mediators of literacy. In B. V. Street (Ed.), *Cross-cultural approaches to literacy* (pp. 294–314). Cambridge: Cambridge University Press.

Beatty, P. (2000). *Lupita mañana.* New York: HarperTrophy.

Bebell, D. (2005). *Technology promoting student excellence: An investigation of the first year of 1:1 computing in New Hampshire middle schools.* Retrieved February 2, 2006, from http://www.bc.edu/research/intasc/PDF/

NH1to1_2004.pdf

Becker, H. J. (2000a). Findings from the Teaching, Learning, and Computing survey: Is Larry Cuban right? *Educational Policy Analysis Archives, 8*(51). Retrieved March 23, 2006, from http://epaa.asu-edu/epaa/

Becker, H. J. (2000b). Who's wired and who's not? *The Future of Children, 10*(2), 44–75.

Black, R. (2005). Access and affiliation: The literacy and composition practices of English langauge learners in an online fanfiction community. *Journal of Adolescent and Adult Literacy, 49*(2), 118–128.

Black, R. W. (in press). Just don't call them cartoons: Anime, manga, fanfiction, and new literacies. In J. Leu, J. Donald, J. Coiro, C. Lankshear, & M. Knobel (Eds.), *Handbook of research on new literacies.* Mahwah, NJ: Lawrence Erlbaum.

Blackboard. (2005). *Welcome to Blackboard.* Retrieved February 2, 2006, from http://www.blackboard.com

Bobrowsky, W. I., Vath, R., Soloway, E., Krajcik, J., & Blumenfeld, P. (2004, April). *The Palm project: The impact of handhelds on science learning in seventh grade.* Paper presented at the annual meeting of the American Educational Research Association, San Diego, CA.

Bolter, J. D. (1991). *Writing space: The computer, hypertext, and the history of writing.* Hillsdale, NJ: Lawrence Erlbaum.

Bourdieu, P. (1986). The forms of capital. In J. G. Richardson (Ed.), *Handbook of theory and research for the sociology of education* (pp. 241–258). New York: Greenwood Press.

Bourdieu, P., & Passeron, J.-C. (1986). *Reproduction in education, society, and culture.* London: Sage.

BrainPOP. (2005). *BrainPop—Health, science, technology, math, English animation and educational site for kids.* Retrieved February 2, 2006, from http://www.brainpop.com

British Education Communications and Technology Agency. (2004). *Handheld computers in schools.* Conventry, UK: Author.

Brown, C. G., Rocha, E., Sharkey, A., Hadley, E., Handley, C., & Kronley, R. A. (2005). *Getting smarter, becoming fairer: A progressive education agenda for a stronger nation.* Washington: Center for American Progress and Institute for America's Future.

Brown, J. S., & Duguid, P. (2000). *The social life of information.* Boston: Harvard Business School Press.

Bureau of Labor Statistics. (2005). *Tomorrow's jobs.* Retrieved February 2, 2006, from http://www.bls.gov/oco/oco2003.htm

Burstein, J. C. (2003). The e-rater scoring engine: Automated essay scoring with natural language processing. In M. D. Shermis & J. C. Burstein (Eds.), *Automated essay scoring: A cross-disciplinary perspective* (pp. 113–121). Mahwah, NJ: Lawrence Erlbaum.

Cagle, D. (2006). *Daryl Cagle's professional cartoonists' index.* Retrieved February 2, 2006, from http://cagle.msnbc.com

Campaign for Tobacco-Free Kids. (2006). *Campaign for Tobacco-Free Kids.* Retrieved February 2, 2006, from http://tobaccofreekids.org

Castells, M. (1996). *The rise of the network society.* Malden, MA: Blackwell.

Castells, M. (1999). *Information technology, globalization and social development.* Geneva: United Nations Research Institute for Social Development:.

Center for Digital Storytelling. (2005). Understanding digital storytelling. Retrieved February 2, 2006, from http://www.storycenter.org/understanding.html

Center for Education Policy, Applied Research, and Evaluation. (2005). *CEPARE Publications—Maine Learning Technology Initiative.* Retrieved February 2, 2006, from http://www.usm.maine.edu/cepare/mlti.htm

Chall, J. S. (1996). *Stages of reading development* (2nd Ed.). Fort Worth, TX: Harcourt Brace College Publishers.

Chall, J. S., Jacobs, V. A., & Baldwin, L. E. (1990). *The reading crisis: Why poor children fall behind.* Cambridge, MA: Harvard University Press.

Cheville, J. (2004). Automated scoring technologies and the rising influence of error. *English Journal, 93*(4), 47–52.

Christen, W. L., & Murphy, T. J. (1991). *Increasing comprehension by activating prior knowledge.* Retrieved February 2, 2006, from http://reading.indiana.edu/ieo/digests/d61.html

Coding Monkeys. (2005). *SubEthaEdit: Collaborative text editing.* Retrieved February 2, 2006, from http://www.codingmonkeys.de/subethaedit/

Coerr, E. (1999). *Sadako and the thousand paper cranes.* New York: Puffin Books.

Columbus Medical Association Foundation. (2006). *Open heart.* Retrieved February 2, 2006, from http://www.cosi.org/onlineExhibits/openHeart/heart.html

Computer Economics. (2005). *Falling costs of mobile computing drive corporate adoption.* Retrieved February 2, 2006, from http://www.computereconomics.com/article.cfm?id=1086/

ComScore Networks. (2005). *Behaviors of the blogosphere: Understanding the scale, composition, and activities of Weblog audiences.* Retrieved February 2, 2006, from http://www.comscore.com/blogreport/comScoreBlogReport.pdf

Conference on College Composition and Communication. (2004). *CCCC position statement on teaching, learning, and assessing writing in digital environments.* Retrieved February 2, 2006, from http://www.ncte.org/groups/cccc/positions/115775.htm

Connell, J. P., & Wellborn, J. G. (1990). Competence, autonomy, and relatedness: A motivational analysis of self-system processes. In M. Gunnar & L. A. Sroufe (Eds.), *Minnesota symposium on child psychology (Vol. 23).* Chicago: University of Chicago Press.

Cook, T. D., Appleton, H., Conner, R., Shaffer, A., Tamkin, G., & Weber, S. J. (1975). *"Sesame Street" revisited.* New York: Russell Sage Foundation.

Csikszentmihalyi, M. (1990). *Flow: The psychology of optimal experience.* New York: Harper Perennial.

Cuban, L. (1986). *Teachers and machines: The classroom use of technology since 1920.* New York: Teachers College Press.

Cuban, L. (1993). Computer meets classroom: Classroom wins. *Teachers College Record, 95*(2), 185–210.

Cuban, L. (2001). *Oversold and underused: Computers in classrooms, 1980–2000.* Cambridge: Harvard University Press.

Culp, K. M. M., Honey, M., & Mandinach, E. (2003). *A retrospective on twenty years of education technology policy.* Retrieved February 2, 2006, from http://www.nationaledtechplan.org/participate/20years.pdf

Cummins, J. (1991). Interdependence of first and second language proficiency in bilingual children. In E. Bialystok (Ed.), *Language processing in bilingual children* (pp. 70–89). Cambridge: Cambridge University Press.

Cummins, J. (1998). e-Lective language learning: Design of a computer-assisted text-based ESL/EFL learning system. *TESOL Journal, 7*(3), 18–21.

Cummins, J. (2005). *Technology, literacy, and young second language learners: Designing educational futures.* Retrieved February 2, 2006, from http://www.ucop.edu/elltech/cumminspaper012005.pdf

Curtis, M., Williams, B., Norris, C., O'Leary, D., & Soloway, E. (2003). *Palm handheld computers: A complete resource for classroom teachers.* Eugene, OR: International Society for Technology in Education.

Daley, E. (2003). Expanding the concept of literacy. *EDUCAUSE Review, 38*(2), 32–40.

Davies, A. (2004). *Finding proof of learning in a one-to-one computing classroom.* Courtenay, BC: Connections Publishing.

Day, A., & Miller, M. (1990, September 2). Gabriel Garcia Marquez on the misfortunes of Latin America, his friendship with Fidel Castro and his terror of the blank page. *Los Angeles Times*, p. 10 (magazine).

Day, J. C., & Newburger, E. C. (2002). *The big payoff: Educational attainment and synthetic estimates of work-line earnings.* Washington, DC: Commerce Department, Economics and Statistics Administration, Census Bureau.

Dede, C., Clarke, J., Ketelhut, D. J., Nelson, B., & Bowman, C. (2005, April). Students' motivation and learning of science in a multi-user virtual environment. Paper presented at the annual meeting of the American Educational Research Association, Montreal, Canada.

Dodge, B. (2005). *The WebQuest page.* Retrieved February 2, 2006, from http://webquest.sdsu.edu

Donahue, P., Daane, M., & Grigg, W. (2003). *The nation's report card: Reading highlights 2003.* Washington, DC: National Center for Educational Statistics.

Driver, M. (2000). *Beowulf to Lear: Text, image, and hypertext.* Retrieved February 2, 2006, from http://csis.pace.edu/grendel

Ed-Data. (2005). *State of California Education Profile.* Retrieved February 2, 2006, from http://www.ed-data.k12.ca.us

Educational Testing Service. (2004). *ETS launches ICT literacy assessment, an online measure of student information and communication technology proficiency.* Retrieved February 2, 2006, from http://www.ets.org/news/04110801.html

Eisenstein, E. L. (1979). *The printing press as an agent of change: Communications and cultural transformations in early-modern Europe.* Cambridge: Cambridge University Press.

Elliot, S. (2003). IntelliMetric: From here to validity. In M. D. Shermis & J. C. Burstein (Eds.), *Automated essay scoring: A cross-disciplinary perspective* (pp. 71–86). Mahwah, NJ: Lawrence Erlbaum.

eMarketer. (2004). *Amid woes, e-mail volume continues to grow.* Retrieved February 2, 2006, from https://www.emarketer.com/Article.aspx?1002881/

Engestrom, Y. (1987). *Learning by expanding.* Helsinki: Orienta-Konsultit.

Expeditionary Learning. (2006). *Expeditionary learning: It's the way school should be.* Retrieved February 2, 2006, from http://www.elob.org

Fairclough, N. (Ed.). (1992a). *Critical language awareness.* London: Longman.

Fairclough, N. (1992b). *Discourse and social power.* London: Polity Press.

Feldon, D. (2004). Dispelling a few myths about learning. *UrbanEd, 1* (4), 37–39.

Fix, M. E., & Passel, J. S. (2001). *U.S. immigration at the beginning of the 21st century: Testimony before the Subcommittee on Immigration and Claims Hearing on "The U.S. Population and Immigration" Committee on the Judiciary, U.S. House of Representatives.* Retrieved February 2, 2006, from http://www.urban.org/urlprint.cfm?ID=7321/

Flesch, R. (1955). *Why Johnny can't read—and what you can do about it.* New York: Harper & Brothers.

Flower, L. (1984). Writer-based prose: A cognitive basis for problems in writing. In S. McKay (Ed.), *Composing in a second language* (pp. 16–42). New York: Newbury House.

Forbes, K. J. (2004). *U.S. manufacturing: Challenges and recommendations.* Retrieved February 2, 2006, from http://www.whitehouse.gov/cea/forbes_nabe_usmanufacturing_3–26-042.pdf

Frankerberg, E., Lee, C., & Orfield, G. (2003). *A multiracial society with segregated schools: Are we losing the dream?* Cambridge, MA: Civil Rights Project, Harvard University.

Fredricks, J. A., Blumenfeld, P. C., & Paris, A. H. (2004). School engagement: Potential of the concept, state of the evidence. *Review of Educational Research, 74*(1), 59–109.

Freire, P., & Macedo, D. (1987). *Reading the word and the world.* Hadley, MA: Bergin & Garvey.

Froguts. (2006). *Welcome to Froguts!—virtual dissection software.* Retrieved February 2, 2006, from http://www.froguts.com

Gee, J. P. (2003). *What video games have to teach us about learning and literacy.* New York: Palgrave Macmillan.

Gee, J. P. (2004). *Situated language and learning: A critique of traditional schooling.* New York: Routledge.

Gee, J. P., Hull, G., & Lankshear, C. (1996). *The new work order: Behind the language of new capitalism.* St. Leonards, Australia: Allen & Unwin.

Gonzales, N. E., Moll, L., & Amanti, C. (2005). *Funds of knowledge: Theorizing practices in households, communities, and classrooms.* Mahwah, NJ:

Lawrence Earlbaum.

Goodman, K. S. (1967). Reading: A psycholinguistic guessing game. *Journal of the Reading Specialist, 6*(1), 126–135.

Grant, D. (n.d.). *Fading footprints.* Retrieved February 2, 2006, from http://king.portlandschools.org/documents/fprints/concepts/FootprintsPDF.pdf

Great Maine Schools Project. (2004). *One-to-one laptops in a high school environment.* Portland, ME: Mitchell Institute.

Guthrie, J. T. (2004). Teaching for literacy engagement. *Journal of Literacy Research, 36*, 1–30.

Haney, W. (2000). The myth of the Texas miracle in education. *Educational Policy Analysis Archives, 8*(41). Retrieved March 23, 2006, from http://epaa.asu.edu/epaa

Harnad, S. (1991). Post-Gutenberg galaxy: The fourth revolution in the means of production and knowledge. *Public-Access Computer Systems Review, 2*(1), 39–53.

Harris, W. J., & Smith, L. (2004). *Laptop use by seventh grade students with disabilities: Perceptions of special education teachers.* Retrieved February 2, 2006, from http://www.usm.maine.edu/cepare/pdf/mlti/MLTI%20Phase%20One%20Evaluation%20Report%202.pdf

Hart, B., & Risley, T. R. (1995). *Meaningful differences in the everyday experience of young American children.* Baltimore: Paul H. Brookes.

Healy, J. M. (1998). *Failure to connect: How computers affect our children's minds—and what we can do about it.* New York: Simon & Schuster.

Heath, S. B. (1983). *Ways with words: Language, life, and work in communities and classrooms.* Cambridge: Cambridge University Press.

Howe, H., & Strauss, W. (2000). *Millennials rising: The next great generation.* New York: Vintage Books.

Hull, G. A., & Nelson, M. E. (2005). Locating the semiotic power of multmodality. *Written Communication, 22*(2), 224–261.

Iedema, R. (2001). Resemiotisation. *Semiotica, 137*(1/4), 23–29.

Iedema, R. (2003). Multimodality, resemiotisation: Extending the analysis of discourse as multi-semiotic practice. *Visual Communication, 2*, 29–57.

Indiana Department of Education. (2005). *inACCESS: Affordable Classroom Computers for Every Secondary Student.* Retrieved February 2, 2006, from http://www.doe.state.in.us/technology/inaccess.html

Inspiration Software. (2005). *Inspiration.* Retrieved February 2, 2006, from http://www.inspiration.com/productinfo/inspiration/index.cfm

Intel. (2006). *Intel innovation in education.* Retrieved February 2, 2006, from http://www97.intel.com/education/

International ICT Literacy Panel. (2002). *Digital transformation: A framework for ICT literacy.* Retrieved February 2, 2006, from http://www.ets.org/research/ictliteracy/ictreport.pdf

Intersegmental Committee of the Academic Senates. (2002). *Academic literacy: A statement of competencies expected of students entering California's public colleges and universities.* Sacramento, CA: Author.

Johnson, M. (2003). Digital scholars: The affects [sic] of one-on-one laptop wireless computing on at-risk middle school students. In P. Kommers & G. Richards (Eds.), *Proceedings of World Conference on Educational Multimedia, Hypermedia, and Telecommunications, 2003* (pp. 2413–2416). Chesapeake, VA: Association for the Advancement of Computing in Education.

Johnstone, B. (2003). *Never mind the laptops: Kids, computers, and the transformation of learning.* Lincoln, NE: iUniverse.

Joyce, F. (2005). Fate of the union. Retrieved February 2, 2006, from http://www.alternet.org/story/21312/

Kalyuga, S., Ayres, P., Chandler, P., & Sweller, J. (2003). Expertise reversal effect. *Educational Psychologist, 38*(1), 23–31.

Kaplan, N. (1995). E-literacies: Politexts, hypertexts, and other cultural formations in the late age of print. *Computer-Mediated Communication Magazine, 2*(3), 3–35. Retrieved March 23, 2006, from http://www.december.com/cmc/mag/

Kendall, J. (Ed.). (1990). *Combining service and learning: A resource book for community and service learning.* Raleigh: National Society for Internships and Experiential Education.

Klein, S. P., Hamilton, L. S., McCaffrey, D. F., & Stecher, B. B. (2000). What do test scores in Texas tell us? *Educational Policy Analysis Archives, 8*(49). Retrieved March 23, 2006, from http://epaa.asu.edu/epaa

Knowles, W. T. (2003). The Maine economy through a different lens. *Maine Policy Review, 12*(3), 36–46.

Kozol, J. (1991). *Savage inequalities.* New York: Harper Collins.

Kozol, J. (2005). *The shame of the nation: The restoration of apartheid schooling in America.* New York: Random House.

Krashen, S. (2004). *The power of reading: Insights from the research.* Portsmouth, NH: Heinemann.

Kress, G. (1998). Visual and verbal modes of representation in electronically mediated communication: The potentials of new forms of text. In I. Snyder (Ed.), *Page to screen: Taking literacy into the electronic era* (pp. 53–79). Routledge: London.

Kress, G. (2003). *Literacy in the new media age.* Routledge: London.

Kulik, J. A. (2003). *Effects of using instructional technology in elementary and secondary schools: What controlled evaluation studies say (SRI Project No. P10446.003).* Arlington, VA: SRI International. Retrieved March 23, 2006, from http://www.sri.com/policy/csted/reports/sandt/it/Kulik_IT_in_colleges_and_universities.pdf

Kyle, B. (2000, March 30). Acute pencil shortage strikes state lawmakers. *Bangor Daily News,* p.1.

Lagercrantz, E. (2003). *ClipboardSharing.* Retrieved February 2, 2006, from http://www.lagercrantz.ath.cx/software/clipboardsharing/

Lam, W. S. E. (2005). Second language socialization in a bilingual chat room. *Language Learning and Technology, 8*(3), 44–65.

Landauer, T., Laham, D., & Foltz, P. (2003). Automated scoring and annotation of essays with the Intelligent Essay Assessor. In M. D. Shermis & J. C.

Burstein (Eds.), *Automated essay scoring: A cross-disciplinary perspective* (pp. 87–112). Mahwah, NJ: Lawrence Erlbaum.

Landsberg, M., & Rathi, R. (2005). Elite school will expel AP classes. *Los Angeles Times*, p. B1.

Lardner, J., & Smith, D. (Eds.). (2006). *Inequality matters: The growing economic divide in America and its poisonous consequences.* New York: New Press.

Lenhart, A., & Madden, M. (2005). *Teen content creators and consumers.* Washington, DC: Pew Internet and American Life Project.

Leu, J., Donald J., Kinzer, C. K., Coiro, J., & Cammack, D. M. (2004). Toward a theory of new literacies emerging from the Internet and other information and communication technologies. In R. B. Ruddell & N. Unrau (Eds.), *Theoretical models and processing of reading* (5th ed., pp. 1570–1613). Newark, DE: International Reading Association.

Levin, D., & Arafeh, S. (2002). *The digital disconnect: The widening gap between Internet-savvy students and their schools.* Washington, DC: Pew Internet and American Life Project:.

Levinson, P. (1997). *The soft edge: A natural history and future of the information revolution.* London: Routledge.

Luke, A., & Freebody, P. (1999). A map of possible practices: Further notes on the four resources model. *Practically Primary, 4*(2), 5–8.

Luke, C. (2003). Pedagogy, connectivity, multimodality, and interdisciplinarity. *Reading Research Quarterly, 38*(3), 297–314.

Maine Department of Education. (2005). *MEA 2004–2005 state summary results.* Retrieved February 2, 2006, from http://www.state.me.us/education/mea/0405MEAscores/MEA0405StateResults20JUL05.pdf

Market Data Retrieval. (2004). *Technology in education 2004: A comprehensive report on the state of technology in the K–12 market.* Shelton, CT: Author.

Market Data Retrieval. (2005). *The K–12 technology review 2005.* Shelton, CT: Market Data Retrieval.

Martin, J. R., Christie, F., & Rothery, J. (1994). Social process in education: A reply to Sawyer and Watson (and others). In B. Stierer & J. Maybin (Eds.), *Language, literacy and learning in educational practice* (pp. 232–247). Clevedon, UK: Multilingual Matters.

Mayer, R. E., Blanton, B., Duran, R., & Schustack, M. (1999). *Using new information technlogies in the creation of sustainable afterschool literacy activities: Evaluation of cognitive outcomes.* Retrieved February 2, 2006, from http://www.psych.ucsb.edu/~mayer/fifth_dim_website/HTML/res_reports/final_report.html

McGraw Hill. (2005a). *Open court reading: Level 3.* New York: Author.

McGraw Hill. (2005b). *Open court reading: Level 5.* New York: Author.

McKenzie, J. (2003). One flew over the high school: A review of Todd Oppenheimer's *The Flickering Mind. From Now On, 13*(4). Retrieved March 23, 2006, from http://www.fno.org/dec03/flickering.html

McNeil, L., & Valenzuela, A. (2001). The harmful impact of the TAAS system of testing in Texas: Beneath the accountabilty rhetoric. In G. Orfield & M. Kornhaber (Eds.), *Raising standards or raising barriers? Inequality and high-stakes testing in public education* (pp. 127–150). New York: Century Foundation Press.

McQuillan, J. (1998). *The literacy crisis: False claims, real solutions.* Portsmouth, NH: Heinemann.

Mehan, H. (1985). The structure of classroom discourse. In T. A. van Dijk (Ed.), *Handbook of discourse analysis* (pp. 120–131). London: Academic Press.

Microsoft. (2006). *Microsoft education.* Retrieved February 2, 2006, from http://www.microsoft.com/education/

Miller, J. H. (2002, January). *Get a life! The way we live (now and then).* Paper presented at the Digital Culture Workshop, University of California, Irvine.

MIT Media Lab (2005). *Quanta Computer Inc. to manufacture $100 laptop.* Retrieved February 2, 2006, from http://laptop.media.mit.edu/2005-1213-olpc.html

Moodle. (2005). *Moodle: A free open course management system for online learning.* Retrieved February 2, 2006, from http://moodle.org

National Center for Educational Statistics. (2005). *National trends in reading by performance levels.* Retrieved February 2, 2006, from http://nces.ed.gov/nationsreportcard/ltt/results2004/nat-reading-perf.asp

National Center for Educational Statistics. (2006). *Create a graph.* Retrieved February 2, 2006, from http://nces.ed.gov/nceskids/Graphing/

National Commission on Writing in America's Schools and Colleges. (2003). *The neglected "r": The need for a writing revolution.* New York: College Entrance Examination Board.

New London Group. (1996). A pedagogy of multiliteracies: Designing social futures. *Harvard Educational Review, 66*(1), 60–92.

NoodleTools, Inc. (2006). *NoodleBib.* Retrieved February 2, 2006, from http://www.noodletools.com/tools.html

North Central Regional Educational Laboratory & The Metiri Group. (2003). *enGauge 21st century skills: Literacy in the digital age.* Naperville, IL, and Los Angeles: Authors.

Nye, R. (1968). *Beowulf: A new telling.* New York: Dell.

O'Dwyer, L. M., Russell, M., Bebell, D., & Tucker-Seeley, T. (2005). Examining the relationshiop between home and school computer use and students' English/Language Arts test scores. *Journal of Technology, Learning, and Assessment, 3*(3). Retrieved March 23, 2006, from http://escholarship.bc.edu/jtla

Ong, W. (1982). *Orality and literacy: The technologizing of the word.* London: Routledge.

Oppenheimer, T. (1997). The computer delusion. *Atlantic Monthly, 289*(1), 45–62.

Oppenheimer, T. (2004). *The flickering mind: The false promise of technology in the classroom and how learning can be saved.* New York: Random House.

Orfield, G., Losen, D. J., Wald, J., & Swanson, C. (2004). *Losing our future: how minority youth are being left behind by the graduate rate crisis.* Cambridge, MA: Civil Rights Project, Harvard University.

Papert, S. (1980). *Mindstorms: Children, computers, and powerful ideas.* New York: Basic Books.

Parsad, B., Jones, J., & Greene, B. (2005). *Internet access in U.S. public schools and classrooms: 1994–2003.* Washington, DC: National Center for Educational Statistics.

Partnership for 21st Century Skills. (2003). *Learning for the 21st century: A report and mile guide for 21st century skills.* Washington, DC: Author.

Paterson, W. A., Henry, J. J., O'Quin, K., & Ceptrano, M. A. (2003). Investigating the effectiveness of an integrated learning system on early readers. *Reading Research Quarterly, 38*(2), 172–207.

Pearce, C. (2002). Emergent authorship: The next interactive revolution. *Computers & Graphics, 26*(1), 21–29.

Penuel, W. R. (2005). *Research: What it says about 1 to 1 learning.* Cupertino, CA: Apple Computer.

Piaget, J. (1970). *Science of education and the psychology of the child* (D. Coltman, Trans.). New York: Orion Press.

Population Reference Bureau. (2004). *U.S. Hispanic population growing fastest in the South.* Retrieved February 2, 2006, from http://www.prb.org/Template.cfm?Section=PRB&template=/ContentManagement/ContentDisplay.cfm&ContentID=7827/

Postman, N. (1995). *The end of education: Redefining the value of school.* New York: Vintage Books.

Quill Graphics. (2006). *CELLS alive!* Retrieved February 2, 2006, from http://cellsalive.com

Rainie, L., & Horrigan, J. (2005). *A decade of adoption: How the internet has woven itself into American life.* Washington, DC: Pew Internet and American Life Project.

Reeves, D. (2002). *Accountability in action.* Denver, CO: Advanced Learning Press.

Reich, R. (1991). *The work of nations: Preparing ourselves for 21st century capitalism.* New York: Knopf.

Reid, I. (Ed.). (1987). *The place of genre in learning: Current debates.* Geelong, Australia: Deakin University Center for Studies in Literacy Education.

Renaissance Learning. (2004). *Accelerated Reader.* Retrieved February 2, 2006, from http://www.renlearn.com/ar/

ResearchWare, Inc. (2005). *HyperResearch.* Retrieved February 2, 2006, from http://www.researchware.com/hr/index.html

Robertson, D. S. (1998). *The new renaissance: Computers and the next level of civilization.* New York: Oxford University Press.

Rogers, E. M. (1995). *Diffusion of innovations* (4th ed.). New York: Free Press.

Rohman, D. G. (1965). Pre-writing: The stage of discovery in the writing process. *College Composition and Communication, 16*(2), 106–112.

Russell, M., Bebell, D., & Higgins, J. (2004). Laptop learning: A comparison of teaching and learning in upper elementary classrooms equipped with shared carts of laptops and permanent 1:1 laptops. *Journal of Educational Computing Research, 30*(4), 313–330.

Russell, M., & Plati, T. (2002). Does it matter with what I write?: Comparing performance on paper, computer and portable writing devices. *Current Issues in Education, 5*(4). Retrieved March 23, 2006 from http://cie.asu.edu

Rytina, N. F. (2005). *U.S. legal permanent residents: 2004.* Washington, DC: Department of Homeland Security, Office of Immigration Statistics.

Safe Passage. (2006). *Project safe passage.* Retrieved February 2, 2006, from http://www.safepassage.org

Sandholtz, J. H., Ringstaff, C., & Dwyer, D. C. (1997). *Teaching with technology: Creating student-centered classrooms.* New York: Teachers College Press.

Scardamalia, M. (2003). Knowledge Forum (advances beyond CSILE). In C. Bereiter (Ed.), *Learning technology innovation in Canada* [Special Issue on TeleLearning-NCE]. *Journal of Distance Education, 17*(3), 23–28.

Schaumburg, H. (2001, June). *Fostering girls' computer literacy through laptop learning: Can mobile computers help to level out the gender difference?* Paper presented at the National Educational Computing Conference, Chicago, IL.

Schofield, J. W., & Davidson, A. L. (2004). Achieving equality of student Internet access within schools. In A. Eagly, R. Baron, & L. Hamilton (Eds.), *The social psychology of group identity and social conflict* (pp. 97–109). Washington, DC: APA Books.

Scholastic. (2004). *Reading counts!* [Computer software]. New York: Scholastic, Inc.

Scribner, S., & Cole, M. (1981). *The psychology of literacy.* Cambridge, MA: Harvard University Press.

Seiter, E. (2004). Children reporting online: The cultural politics of the computer lab. *Television and New Media, 5*(2), 87–107.

Shermis, M. D., & Burstein, J. C. (2003). Introduction. In M. D. Shermis & J. C. Burstein (Eds.), *Automated essay scoring: A cross-disciplinary perspective.* Mahwah, NJ: Lawrence Erlbaum.

Silvernail, D. L. (2005). *Does Maine's middle school laptop program improve learning? A review of evidence to date.* Portland, ME: Center for Education Policy, Applied Research, and Evaluation.

Silvernail, D. L., & Lane, D. M. M. (2004). *The impact of Maine's one-to-one laptop program on middle school teachers and students* (Research Report No. 1). Portland: Maine Education Policy Research Institute, University of Southern Maine.

Slavin, R. E., & Cheung, A. (2005). A synthesis of research on language of reading instruction for English language learners. *Review of Educational Research, 75*(2), 247–284.

Smart Technologies. (2006). *Smart ideas.* Retrieved February 2, 2006, from http://www2.smarttech.com/st/en-US/Products/SMART+Ideas/

Soloway, E. (2002, April). *Technology will change the promise of learning: Fi-*

nally realizing the promise. Paper presented at the annual meeting of the American Educational Research Association, New Orleans, LA.

Stoll, C. (1995). *Silicone snake oil: Second thoughts on the Information Highway.* New York: Anchor Books.

Stoll, C. (1999). *High-tech heretic: Why computers don't belong in the classroom and other reflections of a computer contrarian.* New York: Doubleday.

Sunderman, G. L., & Kim, J. (2005). *Teacher quality: Equalizing educational opportunity and outcomes.* Cambridge, MA: Civil Rights Project, Harvard University.

Task Force on the Maine Learning Technology Endowment. (2001). *Teaching and learning for tomorrow: A learning technology plan for Maine's future.* Report to the State of Maine, 119th Legislature, 2nd reg. sess. Retrieved April 21, 2006, from http://www.maine.gov/mlti/resources/mlterpt.pdf

Thinkronize. (2006). *NetTrekker.* Retrieved February 2, 2006, from http://www.nettrekker.com

Twentieth Century Fox. (1996). *Romeo & Juliet.* Retrieved February 2, 2006, from http://www.romeoandjuliet.com

Vahey, P., & Crawford, V. (2003). *Palm Education Pioneers Program: Final evaluation report.* Menlo Park, CA: SRI International.

Vantage Learning. (2006). *My Access!* Retrieved February 2, 2006, from http://www.vantagelearning.com

Vásquez, O. A. (2002). *La Clase Mágica: Imagining optimal possibilities in a bilingual community of learners.* Mahwah, NJ: Lawrence Erlbaum.

Vásquez, O. A., Pease-Alvarez, P., & Shannon, S. M. (1994). *Pushing boundaries: Language in a Mexicano community.* Cambridge: Cambridge University Press.

Velastegui, J. (2005). *Handheld computer use in diverse classrooms.* Unpublished doctoral dissertation, University of California, Irvine, Irvine.

Walker, L., Rockman, S., & Chessler, M. (2000). *A more complex picture: Laptop use and impact in the context of changing home and school access.* Retrieved February 2, 2006, from http://www.elob.org

Ware, P., & Warschauer, M. (in press). Hybrid literacy texts and practices in technology-intensive environments. *International Journal of Educational Research.*

Warschauer, M. (1997). Computer-mediated collaborative learning: Theory and practice. *Modern Language Journal, 81*(4), 470–81.

Warschauer, M. (1999). *Electronic literacies: Language, culture, and power in online education.* Mahwah, NJ: Lawrence Erlbaum.

Warschauer, M. (2000a). Technology and school reform: A view from both sides of the track. *Education Policy Analysis Archives, 8*(4). Retrieved March 23, 2006, from http://epaa.asu.edu/epaa

Warschauer, M. (2000b). The changing global economy and the future of English teaching. *TESOL Quarterly, 34,* 511–535.

Warschauer, M. (2003a). Demystifying the digital divide. *Scientific American, 289*(2), 42–47.

Warschauer, M. (2003b). *Technology and social inclusion: Rethinking the digital divide.* Cambridge, MA: MIT Press.

Warschauer, M., & Cook, J. (1999). Service learning and technology in TESOL. *Prospect, 14*(3), 32–39.

Warschauer, M., Grant, D., Del Real, G., & Rousseau, M. (2004). Promoting academic literacy with technology: Successful laptop programs in K–12 schools. *System, 32*(4), 525–537.

Warschauer, M., & Grimes, D. (2005). *First-year evaluation report: Fullerton School District laptop program.* Retrieved February 2, 2006, from http://www.gse.uci.edu/markw/fsd-laptop-year1-eval.pdf

Warschauer, M., Knobel, M., & Stone, L. A. (2004). Technology and equity in schooling: Deconstructing the digital divide. *Educational Policy, 18*(4), 562–588.

Warschauer, M., & Ware, P. (2006). Automated writing evaluation: Defining the classroom research agenda. *Language Teaching Research, 10*(2), 157–180.

Wells, G., & Chang-Wells, G. L. (1992). *Constructing knowledge together.* Portsmouth, NH: Heinemann.

Wenglinsky, H. (1998). *Does it compute?: The relationship between educational technology and student achievement in mathematics.* Retrieved February 2, 2006, from ftp://ftp.ets.org/pub/res/technolog.pdf

Wertsch, J. V. (1991). *Voices of the mind: A sociocultural approach to mediated action.* Cambridge, MA: Harvard University Press.

Windschitl, M., & Sahl, K. (2002). Tracing teachers' use of technology in a laptop computer school: The interplay of teacher beliefs, social dynamics, and institutional culture. *American Educational Research Journal, 39*(1), 165–205.

Yahoo! Movies. (2005). *Trailers and clips.* Retrieved February 2, 2006, from http://movies.yahoo.com/trailers/

Zemelman, S., Daniels, H., & Hyde, A. (1998). *Best practice: New standards for teaching and learning in America's schools.* Portsmouth, NH: Heinemann.

Index

About the Author

Mark Warschauer is Associate Professor of Education and Informatics at the University of California, Irvine and Associate Director for Research of the Ada Byron Research Center for Diversity in Computing and Information Technology. His research focuses on the relationship between technology use and literacy development among culturally and linguistically diverse learners.